Crochet Kawaii Pets

Crochet Kawaii Pets

30 adorable animals to make

Jacki Donhou

CONTENTS

WELCOME

Hello friends and crochet community!

I am excited to introduce my newest book, *Crochet Kawaii Pets*. This collection features adorable plushie patterns made from soft chenille yarns. You'll find lovable designs for domesticated pets like dogs, cats and rabbits, as well as some not-so-cuddly options like tarantulas, snakes, hermit crabs and more.

As a yarn collector and amigurumi designer, I work with a variety of yarns, both natural and synthetic. Starting a new design involves selecting the right yarn type, weight and brand, which can be quite a process. With my extensive yarn collection, the possibilities for designing are endless. For this book, I knew that these kawaii pet patterns had to be created using plush chenille yarn, making them irresistible! To offer a wide range of colour choices for each pattern, I chose two excellent brands: Bella Chenille yarn from Universal Yarn and Parfait Chunky from Premier Yarns. Both provide beautiful yarns of outstanding quality.

This book is designed with beginner crocheters in mind. The patterns are simple yet teach fun techniques that add form and shape to each finished kawaii pet. Plus, these quick and easy patterns are perfect for markets and craft fairs.

I hope you enjoy making these cute and sweet kawaii pets.
Happy ami making!

Jacki

MATERIALS AND TOOLS

These are the materials and tools you will need to complete the kawaii pet projects in this book.

Yarn

Take your time and select the yarn brand and weights that you are comfortable with. For this book, I chose Bella Chenille from Universal Yarn and Parfait Chunky from Premier Yarns. If Bella Chenille is not available, Bunny Baby from Wolans Yarns is a good alternative. These super-bulky-weight polyester yarns are soft to the touch and are my personal preference to produce a squishy, huggable plush toy. But you choose the yarn you prefer.

If you use a different brand or weight of yarn, remember that different yarns will change the size and look of the final amigurumi. Lighter-weight yarns will create smaller amigurumi, and heavier-weighted yarns will create larger finished amigurumi than shown in this book.

Crochet hooks

Crochet hooks come in a range of sizes. Finding the right hook size for your amigurumi project and choice of yarn can be difficult. The larger the hook, the larger your stitches will be. When working with amigurumi patterns, choosing a hook size smaller than recommended on the yarn label is ideal; this results in tighter stitches with smaller holes so the stuffing doesn't show through. For instance, the recommended hook size for both Bella Chenille and Parfait Chunky yarns is 8mm (UK0:US L/11), but this would be for making blankets. The projects in this book require a much tighter stitch, so I went down to a 3.5mm (UK9:US E/4) hook size to guarantee that the stuffing would not show through the stitches.

Safety eyes

Safety eyes are hard plastic eyes with washer backs. They can be found in craft supply stores. They are available in solid colours, multi-colours and even glitter for added sparkle. I have used two sizes of solid black eyes for my patterns: ½in (14mm), and ¾in (18mm). See page 18 for instructions on how to attach them. Please note that if you are making an amigurumi for a young child, it is advisable to embroider the eyes rather than using safety eyes.

Scissors

Using a small pair of embroidery scissors with sharp tips is best. When you need to trim yarn ends after fastening off, smaller scissors lessen the risk of cutting through and damaging the other stitches.

Stuffing

Polyester fibre filling is a synthetic hypoallergenic fibre made for pillows, crafts and toys. When you stuff an amigurumi piece, add the fibre filling in small amounts to control the shaping and size of the amigurumi. You want it to be firm enough to hold its shape but not to be over-stuffed.

Embroidery needles

Embroidery needles are long needles with a large eye used to sew together and attach the amigurumi pieces. With my patterns, I tend to use two needles: a large needle with a blunt tip to sew the body parts together approximately 3½in (9cm) in total length, with an eye 1in (2.5cm) long – and a needle with a sharp tip approximately the same size for the eye details. If you find another size needle that works best for you, use the more comfortable size.

Stitch markers

Stitch markers are plastic or metal clasps that hook onto your crochet work and are designed to keep track of either the starting or the ending stitch in your rounds. As you crochet on from round 1, you can move your stitch marker up to the next round.

Sewing pins

Use these stick pins to keep all your amigurumi body parts secured and in place for sewing. Pins with a ball or a heart on the top are easier to use and give you something to hold. They are also easier to see against the crocheted surface. Pins with a flat top are not recommended, because they can get lost in your amigurumi pieces. I like to use a lot of pins, so my pieces stay in the correct place and do not move while I am attaching them.

Poly pellets

Poly pellets are little plastic pellets or beads that can be used to make a weighted base for a crochet amigurumi project. The weight helps to make the pet sit or stand upright. Since the pellets are small enough to eventually work their way through the spaces between the crochet stitches, they need to be placed inside a small nylon stocking to stay within the amigurumi project. Only fill the stocking with a few pellets. If the stocking will not fit, remove some of the pellets. Then tightly secure both ends of the stocking before placing it in the base of the amigurumi. Add stuffing as normal. Poly pellets are not recommended for toys for children under three.

STITCHES AND TECHNIQUES

Here we explain the crochet stitches and techniques you will need to be familiar with to make the projects in this book. With easy-to-follow instructions and clear illustrations, you'll be making the most fabulous amigurumi pets in no time.

Holding a hook

To hold a crochet hook, use your dominant hand to grip the hook and your less dominant hand for holding the yarn.

Hold the crochet hook at a downward angle, like a knife.

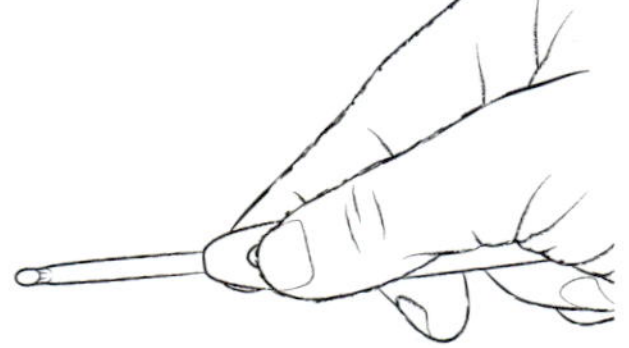

Holding yarn

There are many ways to hold the yarn while you crochet. It all depends on which hold is the most comfortable for you to maintain the right amount of tension.

If the yarn tension is too tight as you crochet, inserting the crochet hook in the next set of stitches could be difficult. If the tension is too loose, you will create holes in the rounds through which the stuffing could show. Take the time to find a hold that suits you.

Step 1: A simple way to hold the yarn is to begin by wrapping it around your little finger, then carry it under the next two fingers and over the index finger.

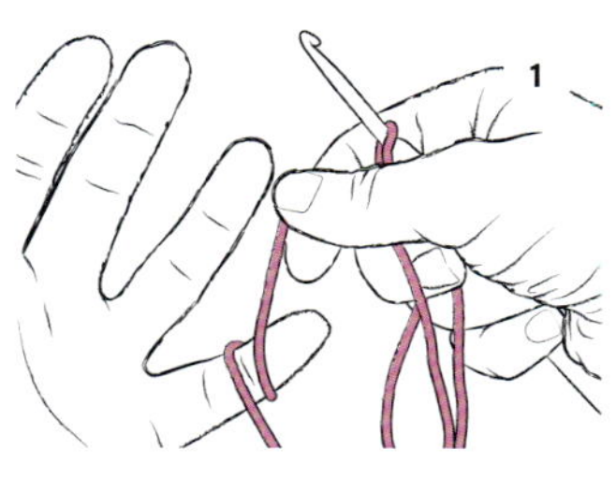

Step 2: Your thumb and middle finger will then grip the tail end of the yarn to hold it in place. Elevate your index finger to add the tension the yarn needs and make your first stitch.

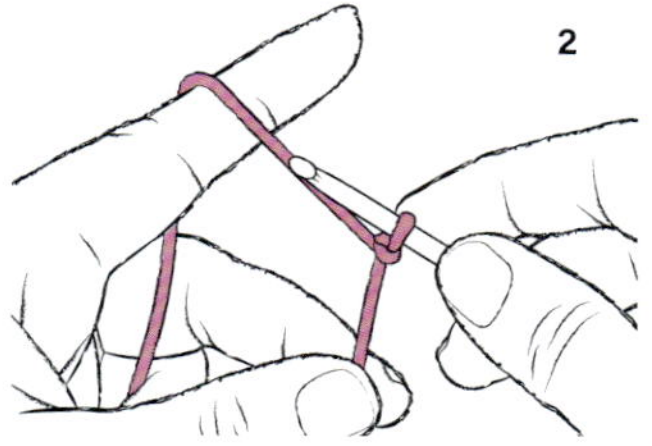

Making a slipknot

Almost all pieces of crochet begin with a slipknot.

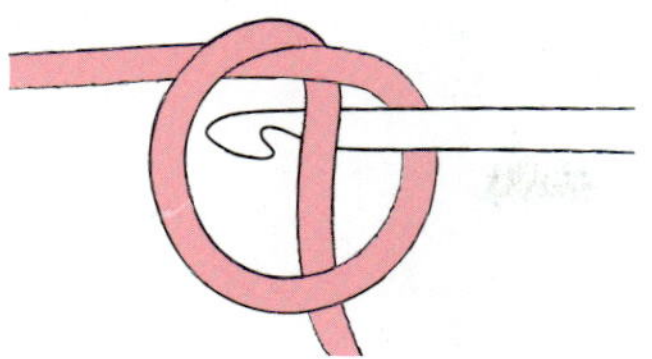

Holding the yarn end, make a loop by crossing the yarn over itself. Insert the hook through the centre of the loop, yarn over the hook and pull the hook back through the centre. Pull the yarn end to tighten the loop on the hook to create the slipknot.

Chain stitch (ch)

A chain stitch is a basic stitch that is mostly used to start or end a row.

Step 1: Starting with a slipknot, wrap the yarn around the crochet hook.

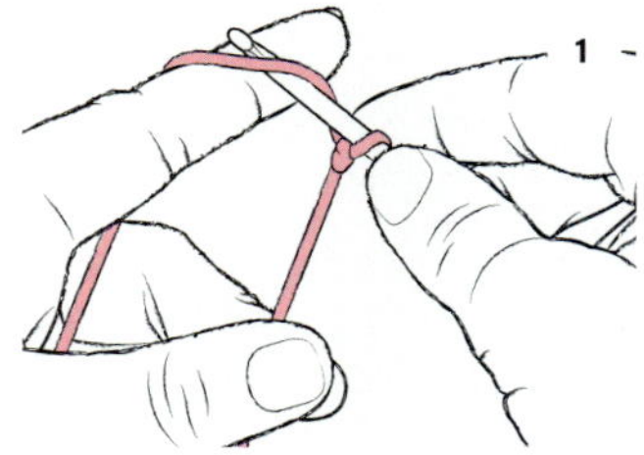

Step 2: Simply pull the yarn through the loop on the hook to form the first chain.

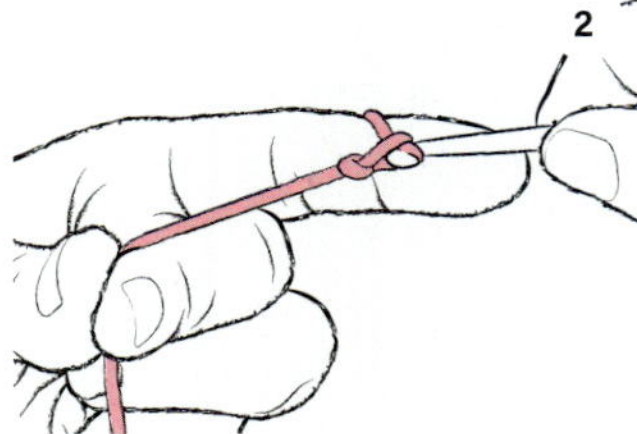

Step 3: If you need to make several chain stitches, repeat the steps until you have the required number.

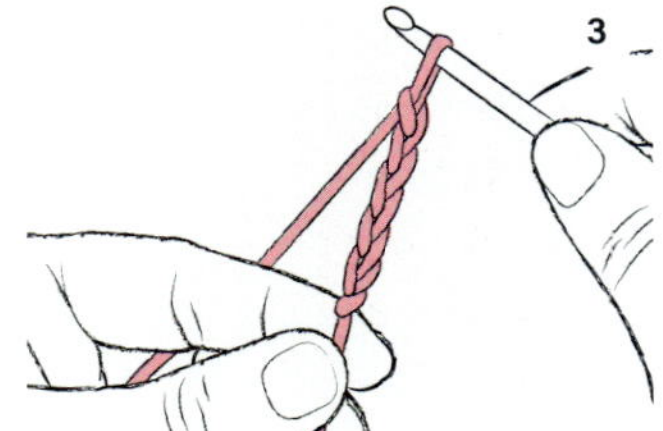

Slip stitch (sl st)

The slip stitch has more than one use in a pattern, adding a detailed seam to a piece and sometimes connecting pieces together.

Step 1: Insert the crochet hook under the stitch and wrap the yarn around the crochet hook.

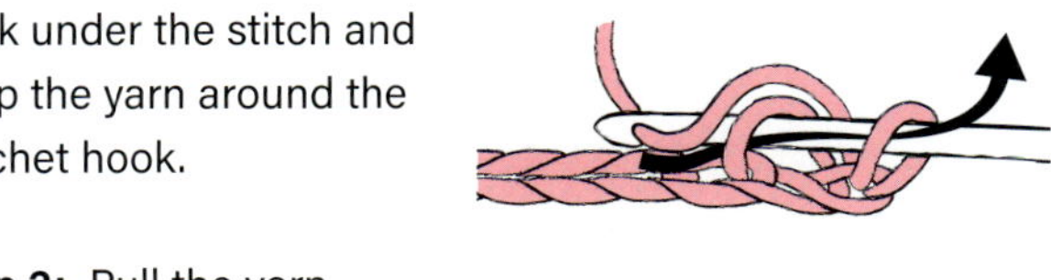

Step 2: Pull the yarn through the stitch and through the loop on the crochet hook. If you need to make several slip stitches, repeat the steps until you have the number of slip stitches for the pattern.

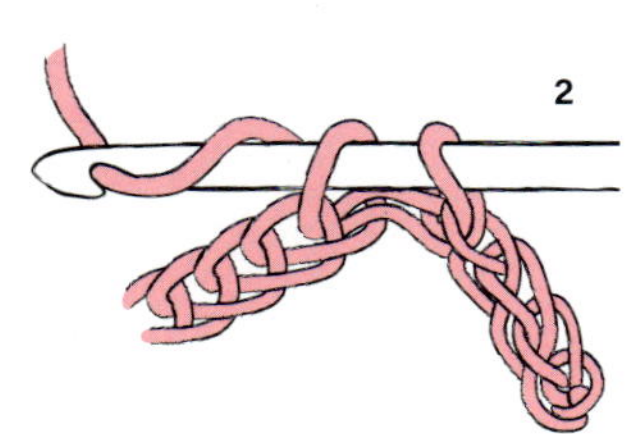

Double crochet (dc)

Double crochet is the main stitch used for the projects.

Step 1: Insert the crochet hook under both loops of the stitch or the chain space.

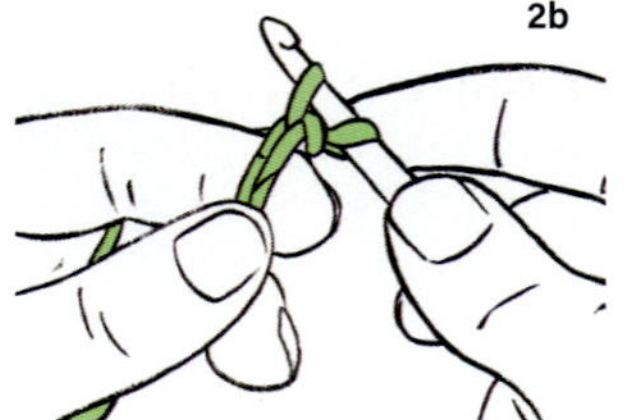

Step 2: Wrap the yarn around the crochet hook and pull the yarn through the stitch. There will be two loops on the crochet hook.

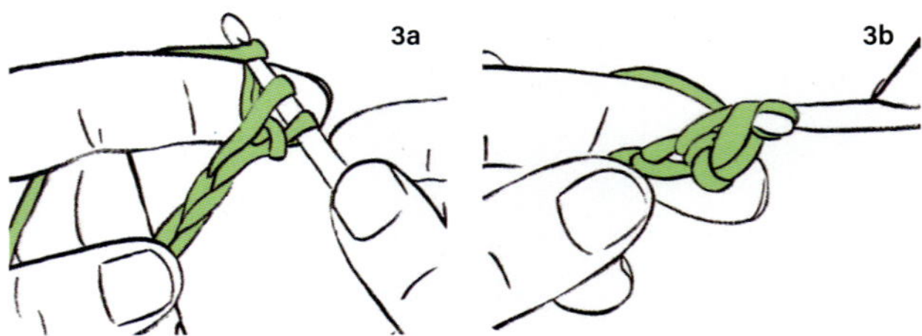

Step 3: Wrap the yarn around the crochet hook once more and pull the yarn through both loops on the crochet hook.

Treble (tr)

Treble stitch is a taller version of double crochet.

Step 1: Wrap the yarn around the crochet hook and then insert the hook under the stitch or the chain space.

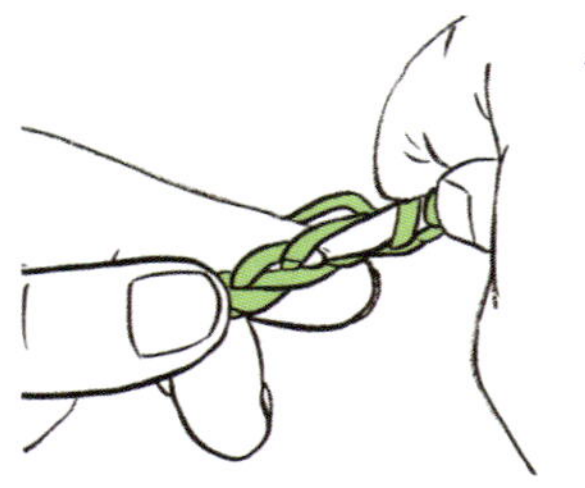

Step 2: Wrap the yarn around the crochet hook and pull the yarn through the stitch. There will be three loops on the crochet hook. Wrap the yarn around the crochet hook again.

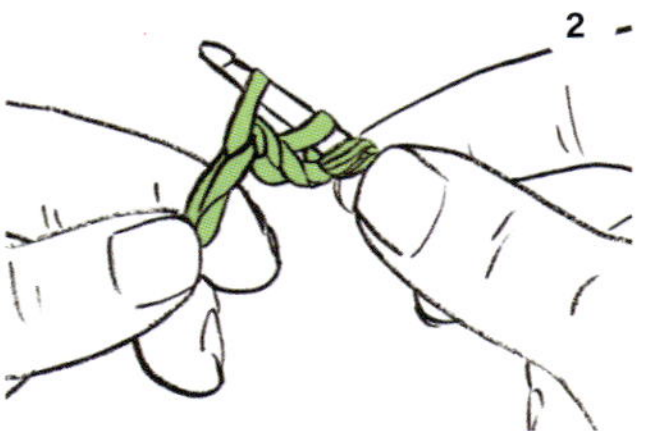

Step 3: Pull the yarn through two of the loops on the crochet hook, leaving two loops on the crochet hook. Then, wrap the yarn around the hook once more.

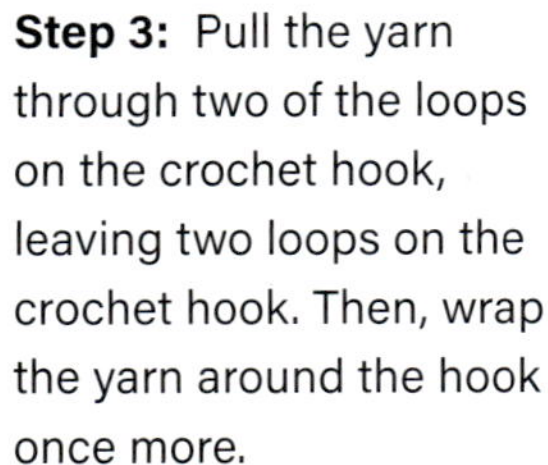

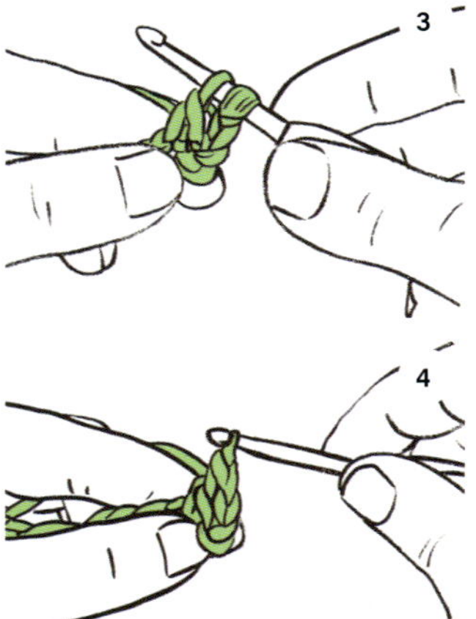

Step 4: Pull the yarn through the last two remaining loops on the crochet hook.

Third loop

The third loop of a double crochet stitch is on the back side of the row and below the back loop. It runs horizontally like a line or bar behind the stitch. Grab this loop with the point of the hook rather than pushing the hook under the loop; it makes it easier in case the tension is tighter.

Half treble (htr)

Half treble stitch is similar to double crochet but starts by wrapping the yarn around the crochet hook at the beginning of the stitch.

Step 1: Wrap the yarn around the crochet hook, then insert the hook under the stitch or the chain space.

Step 2: Wrap the yarn around the crochet hook and pull the yarn through the stitch. There will be three loops on the crochet hook.

Step 3: Wrap the yarn around the crochet hook once more and pull the yarn through all three loops on the crochet hook.

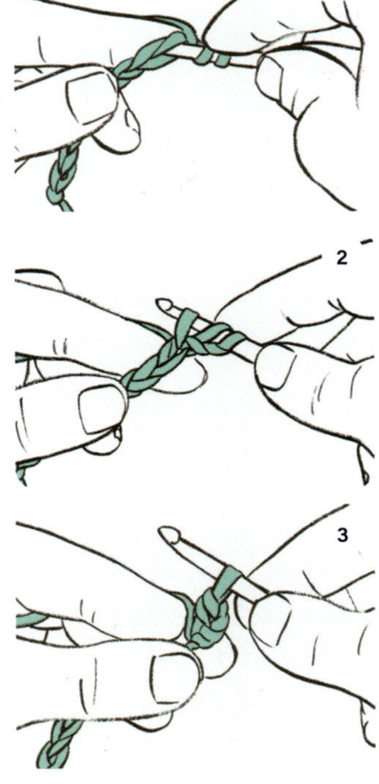

Double treble (dtr)

Double treble stitch is an even taller stitch that starts by wrapping the yarn around the crochet hook two times at the beginning of the stitch.

Step 1: Wrap the yarn around the crochet hook twice and then insert the hook under the stitch or the chain space.

Step 2: Wrap the yarn around the crochet hook and pull the yarn through the stitch. There will be four loops on the crochet hook.

Step 3: Wrap the yarn around the crochet hook again and pull the yarn through two of the four loops on the crochet hook. This will leave three loops on the crochet hook. Wrap the yarn around the crochet hook and pull the yarn through two of the three loops on the crochet hook, leaving two loops on the crochet hook.

Step 4: Wrap the yarn around the crochet hook once more and pull the yarn through the last two loops on the crochet hook to complete the stitch.

Work 2 double crochet stitches into the next stitch to increase (dc2inc)

Working two stitches in the same space is a way to make a row or round larger (known as increasing).

Work two double crochet stitches in the same stitch or chain space. This will increase the stitch count by one stitch.

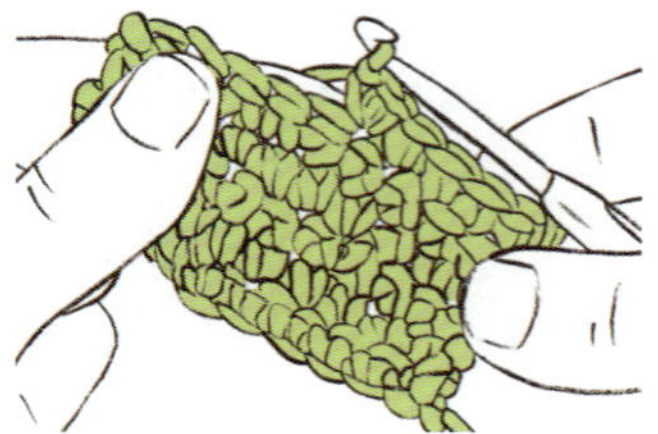

Work 2 double treble stitches into the next stitch to increase (dtr2inc)

Another way to increase a row or a round is to use two double treble stitches.

Work two double treble stitches in the same stitch or chain space. This will increase the stitch count by one stitch.

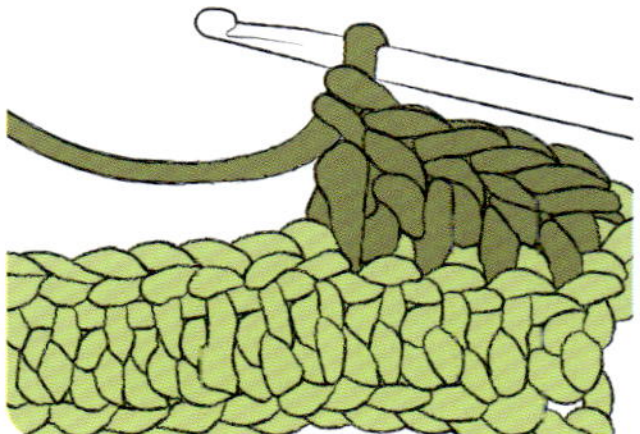

Work 2 half treble stitches into the next stitch to increase (htr2inc)

Another way to increase a row or a round is to use two half treble stitches.

Work two half treble stitches in the same stitch or chain space. This will increase the stitch count by one stitch.

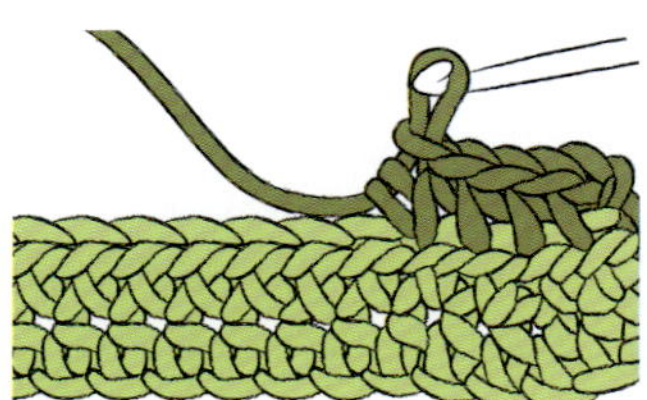

Work 2 double crochet stitches together to decrease (dc2tog)

A decrease means crocheting two stitches together to shorten a row or round. The method shown here is for an invisible decrease, where the front loops of the two stitches are pulled together so that the back loops collapse behind the stitch to close up the small hole and prevent the stuffing from showing.

Step 1: Insert the hook under the front loop only of the stitch. Then, insert the hook under the front loop only of the next stitch.

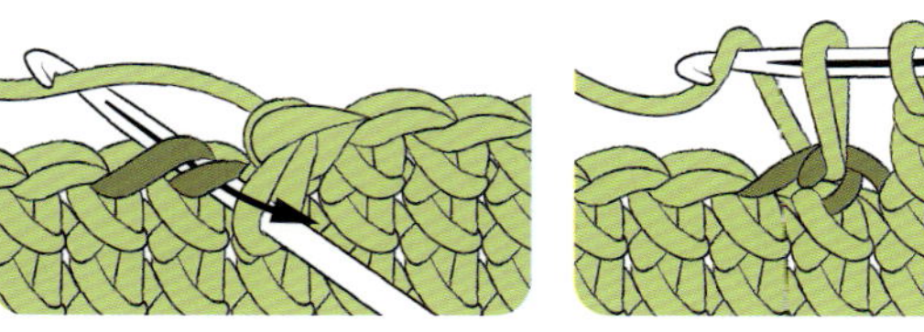

Step 2: With three loops on the hook, wrap the yarn around the crochet hook and pull through both the front loops. This leaves two loops left on the hook. Wrap the yarn around the hook and pull through the last two loops.

Magic circle (MC)

The magic circle or ring is the cleanest way to begin a round when crocheting, especially when making amigurumi. It is an adjustable ring with an end, usually made with double crochet stitches, that tightens to close the centre of the first round.

Step 1: Holding the yarn end, make a loop by crossing the yarn over itself. Then, grip that crossing point, insert the hook through the centre of the loop, wrap the yarn around the crochet hook, and pull the hook back through the centre.

Step 2: While still holding the circle, wrap the yarn around the crochet hook and pull the yarn through the loop on the hook to form the first chain. This step is worked around the circle.

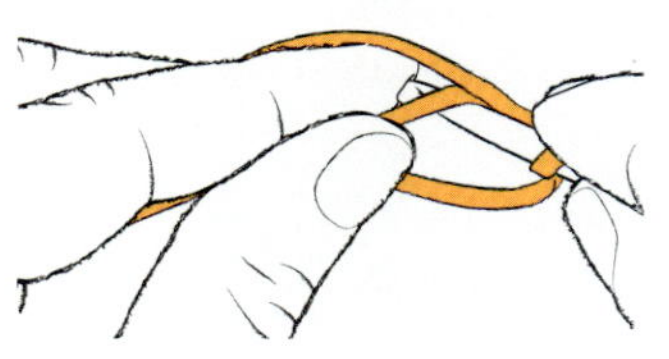

Step 3: Insert the crochet hook through the circle, wrap the yarn around the hook and pull the yarn through. There will be two loops on the crochet hook.

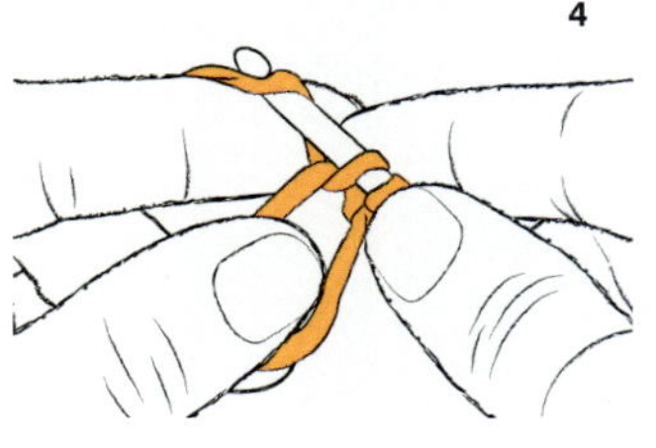

Step 4: Wrap the yarn around the crochet hook once more and pull the yarn through both loops on the crochet hook.

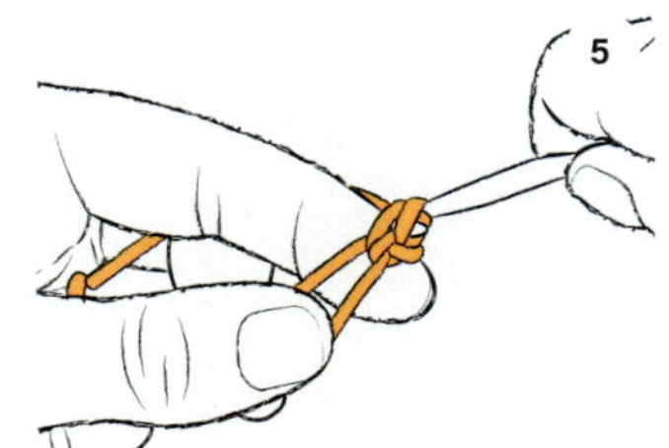

Step 5: This completes the first double crochet stitch on the magic circle. Repeat the steps until you have the number of double crochet stitches for the pattern.

Step 6: Gently pull the yarn end to tighten and close the magic circle. Read the patterns closely, as a few pieces like the ears on some of the pets will instruct you not to close the magic circle at the end.

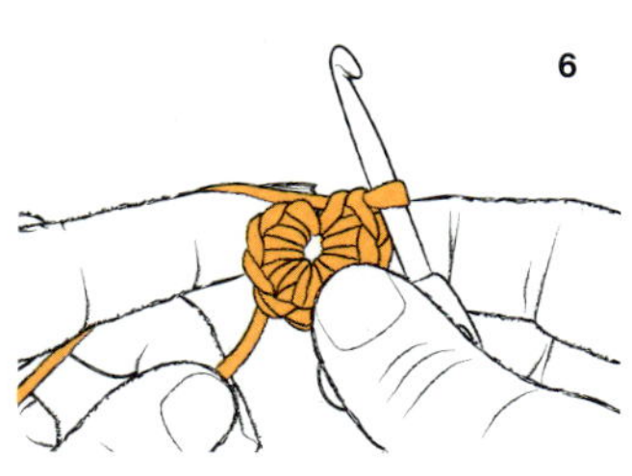

Back loop only (BLO)

The top of a stitch has two loops, a front loop and a back loop. The back loop is the loop that is further from you and the only loop the crochet hook will work under, leaving the closer loop, the front loop, unworked. When working in the back loop only, it changes the effect of the piece you are working on. It reshapes your work and forces the stitches back from their original position. Insert the hook under the loop of the next stitch that is further away, not under both loops of the next stitch.

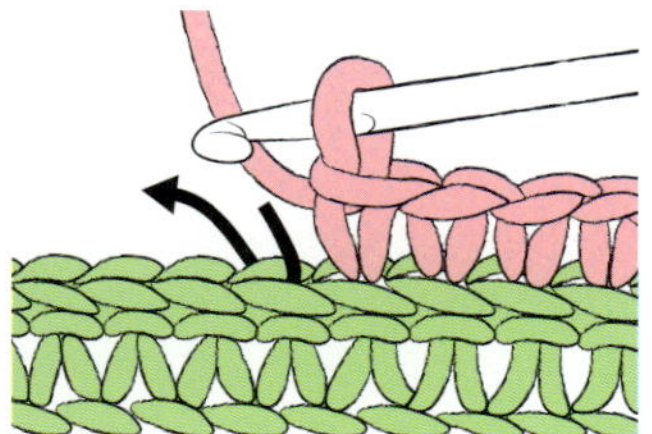

Front loop only (FLO)

The front loop of the stitch is the loop that is closer to you and the only loop the crochet hook will work under, leaving the BLO unworked. When working FLO stitches, it changes the positioning of the stitches and curves your next rounds or rows forward. This technique is also used when closing up a piece made from bottom to top by tightening up the last round. Insert the hook under the loop of the next stitch that is nearer you, not under both loops of the next stitch.

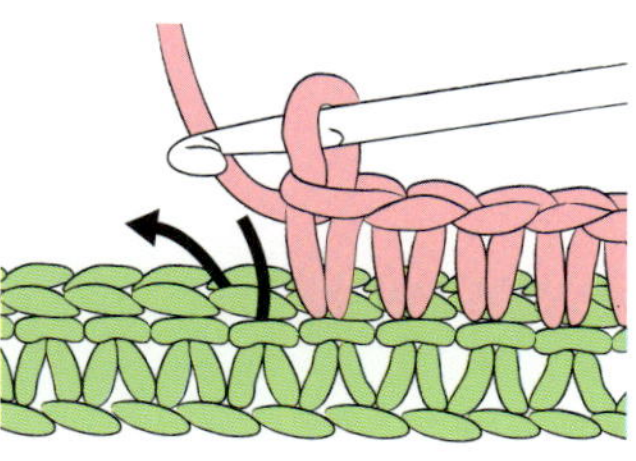

Bobble stitch (BOB)

Bobble stitches are little puffy balls crocheted into the pattern to add toes and thumbs. They are made from six unfinished treble crochet left on the hook within the same stitch and then closed at the end.

Step 1: Yarn over and insert the hook under the next stitch. Yarn over and pull through the stitch, yarn over again and pull through two stitches. Repeat these steps five times until there are six loops on the hook.

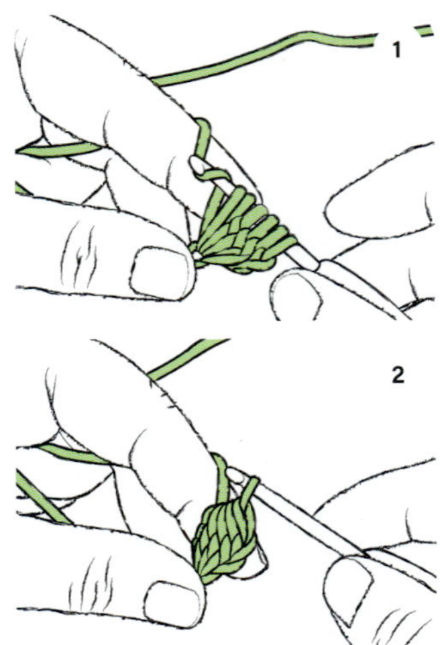

Step 2: Yarn over and pull through all six loops.

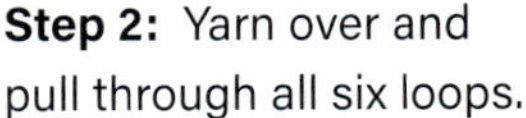

Changing colours

When working on a pattern using multiple-colour yarns, colour changes within the rounds are necessary.

Step 1: When you need to change a colour in a round, leave the last stitch of the previous colour unfinished, without pulling the final loop through the stitch.

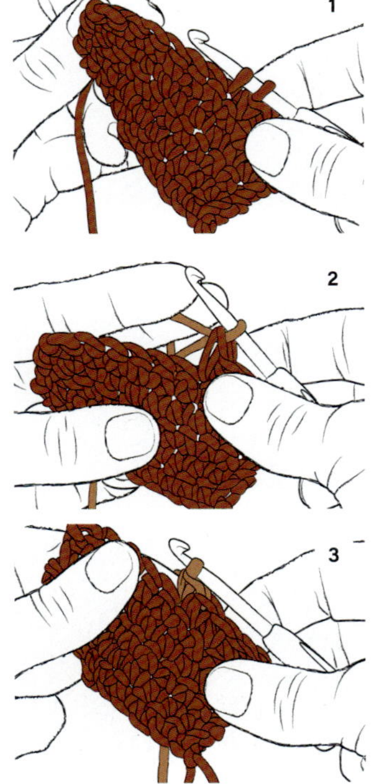

Step 2: Wrap the new colour around the hook and pull through the leftover loops.

Step 3: Continue the new colour in the next stitch or stitches. Tie the loose tails in a knot and leave them inside the crocheted piece.

Yarn over and yarn under

There is no right or wrong way to make your stitches – you can use either yarn over or yarn under. It just comes down to what you are more comfortable with.

Yarn over happens when you hook the yarn strand from underneath, forcing the yarn on top of the hook. When pulled through the stitch to make a double crochet, the result looks like a V-shape.

Yarn under happens when you hook the top of the yarn strand, wrapping it under the hook. When pulled through the stitch to make a double crochet, the result looks like an X-shape.

Working with yarn under, the stitches come out tighter, with fewer holes between them, resulting in a small amigurumi. The yarn over technique has the opposite effect: the stitches will come out slightly larger, which makes the amigurumi pieces bigger.

Invisible fasten off in a round

Fastening off in a round can leave a noticeable bump, whereas an invisible fasten off will make a cleaner finish to the round.

Step 1: Cut the end of the yarn, leaving a yarn tail of about 4in (10cm). Pull the loop up and out of the last stitch.

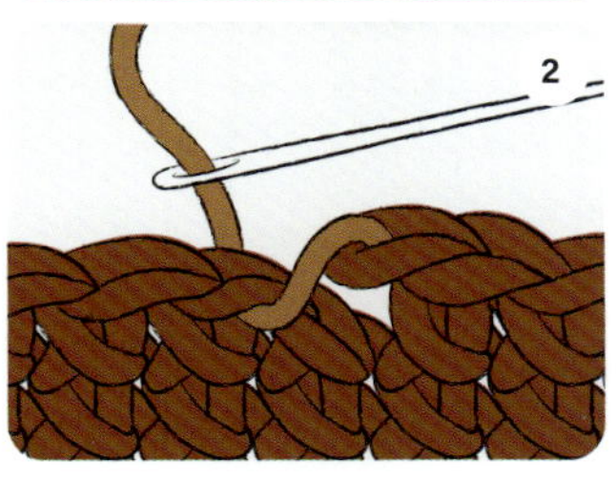

Step 2: With a large embroidery needle, thread the tail through the eye of the needle. Before moving on, count the stitches in the round backwards and mark the first stitch of that round. Insert the needle under both of the top loops of the second stitch that is next to the marked stitch. This will overlap the first stitch, ensuring that you keep the same number of stitches in the round.

Step 3: Pull the needle up and insert it underneath the back loop of the last stitch in the round. This is the same stitch the yarn started from. Weave in the tail on the back or inside of the piece.

Fasten off in a row

Fastening off at the end of a row is very important. Leaving the tail end of the yarn exposed or loose can result in the piece unravelling and you losing all your hard work. Always fasten off properly to prevent that from happening.

Cut the end of the yarn, leaving a yarn tail of about 4in (10cm). Pull the tail up through the loop with the hook.

Weaving in the ends after sewing

Weaving in the loose ends is usually the final step in any crochet project. It can seem like a lot of work. To avoid feeling overwhelmed, it is best to weave in a few of the ends as you sew the pieces together.

Step 1: Thread a large embroidery needle with the end or yarn tail, then insert the needle through the amigurumi piece and out at an inconspicuous location. Insert the needle underneath a few stitches along one of the rows or rounds.

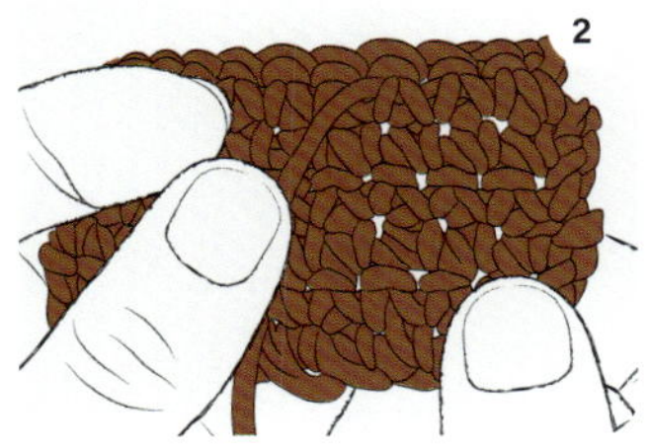

Step 2: Pull the yarn slightly tight and then reverse to come back in the other direction under a few more stitches. Hide the remaining yarn tail in the amigurumi piece.

Step 3 (optional): When working with chenille yarn, if step 2 becomes difficult, resulting in the yarn shredding or falling apart, weave the yarn back and forth through the centre of the piece a few times. This will wrap the yarn tail around the stuffing. Hide the remaining yarn tail in the amigurumi piece.

FINISHING TOUCHES

This next section will teach you how to sew all the pieces together and add special details to your kawaii pets. It is the last step of completing your amigurumi so you can now be proud of your accomplishments.

Whip stitch

Whip stitch is used to attach the body parts together.

First, make sure the two pieces are pinned against each other in the location the pattern states. Thread a large embroidery needle with the leftover tail of the first piece being attached and insert the needle under the stitch of the matched-up stitch on the second piece and pull it through. Next, bring the needle back up and under both loops of the next stitch on the piece that is being attached and pull the yarn tight. Then insert the needle under the next stitch of the second piece. Repeat the steps until the pieces are securely attached.

To add whip stitches to noses or cheeks, use a small embroidery needle. Insert the needle in the first location stated in the instructions and out at the second location. Repeat the steps until the number of whip stitches needed have been completed.

Adding safety eyes

Note that safety eyes can be dangerous if removed by a small child. For young children, embroider the eyes instead.

Place the stem of the black safety eye through the skipped stitch on the round indicated in the pattern. With the stem exposed on the inside of the crocheted head, firmly push the washer over the stem until it clicks into place. The tighter the washer is against the back side of the safety eye, the less chance the eye details will slip under them.

If you are working with curved or cup-shaped washers, make sure the open cup side of the washer is placed on the stem first. This will sink the eye into the washer and help to prevent it from falling off.

If the location of the safety eyes in the pattern is not centred on the face of the kawaii pet, adjust the eyes left or right by 1–2 stitches to achieve the correct placement. Variations in tension and yarn weight can cause the safety eyes to be misaligned.

Outlining the safety eyes

Safety eyes on amigurumi are usually solid black with a dull matt finish. Outlining the eyes gives the amigurumi realistic features by adding a sweet expression. The position of the eye outlines and cheek details vary according to the pattern to give slightly different facial expressions. Make sure you follow the pattern photos for guidance.

Using white yarn and a needle with a sharp tip, push the needle through the side of the head and out at the outside of the first eye. Then insert the needle back through the bottom of the eye. Pull the needle through the head and out the stitch you entered. This adds a stripe to the outer portion of the eye. Tie the ends together and hide them inside the head. Then repeat the steps for the second eye.

Adding cheeks

With pink yarn, push the needle through the side of the head and out under the bottom of the white outline of the first eye. Follow the pattern photos for guidance. Insert your needle back through the side of the head 1.5 to 2 stitches away and then back up through the bottom of the eye. Repeat this step to create 2 whip stitches for the cheek. Push the needle through the head and out through the first stitch. Tie the ends together and hide them inside the head. Then repeat the steps for the second eye.

ABBREVIATIONS

The patterns in this book are written in UK crochet terms.

( )	repeated/stitch count
BLO	back loop only
BOB	bobble stitch
ch	chain
dc	double crochet
dc2inc	work 2 double crochet into the next stitch to increase
dc2tog	work 2 double crochet stitches together to decrease
dtr	double treble
FLO	front loop only
htr	half treble crochet
htr2inc	work 2 half treble crochet into the next stitch to increase
MC	magic circle
sl st	slip stitch
st or sts	stitch/es
tr	treble crochet
tr2inc	work 2 treble crochet into the next stitch to increase

CASTELLO THE CHAMELEON

The chameleon changes colours based on its moods, surrounding temperature and humidity. Its eyes can move independently in all directions, making it easy to see behind. Our chameleon, Castello, is in a green mood here, possibly because he's feeling chilled, but you could make him in any colour!

Finished size

4in (10cm)

Supplies and materials

- Universal Yarn Bella Chenille, Super Bulky Weight, 100% Polyester, 131yds (120m) per 100g ball
  Yarn A Lime 110
  Yarn B Lapis 126
- Hook size: 3.5mm (UK9:USE/4)
- 2 safety eyes ½in (14mm)
- Polyester fibre filling
- Embroidery needle
- Scissors
- Stitch markers
- Sewing pins

CHAMELEON

Using A, work all stitches in a round from front to back. Stuff as you crochet.

Round 1: Make a MC with 6 dc (6 sts).
Round 2: (Dc2inc) 6 times (12 sts).
Round 3: Dc 3, (dc2inc) 6 times, dc 3 (18 sts).
Round 4: Dc in each st around (18 sts).

Mark stitches 7 and 16 in round 4. These will be the 2 stitches where you will place the safety eyes later in the pattern.

Round 5: Dc 7, (dc2inc) 6 times, dc 5 (24 sts).
Round 6: Dc in each st around (24 sts).

Add the safety eyes in the marked stitches on round 4. There should be 9 stitches between them.

Round 7: Dc 10, (dc2inc) 6 times, dc 8 (30 sts).
Round 8: Dc in each st around (30 sts).
Round 9: (Dc2tog) twice, dc 8, (dc2tog) 4 times, dc 10 (24 sts).
Round 10: Dc 6, (dc2tog) 6 times, dc 4, BOB, dc (18 sts).
Round 11: Dc 2, BOB, dc 15 (18 sts).
Round 12: Dc 4, (dc2inc, dc) 5 times, dc2inc, dc 3 (24 sts).
Round 13: (Dc 3, dc2inc) 6 times (30 sts).

If the decreases in the next rounds are not centred on the back, adjust the dc2tog stitches by 1–2 stitches.

Round 14: Dc 13, (dc2tog) 3 times, dc 11 (27 sts).
Round 15: Dc in each st around (27 sts).
Round 16: Dc 12, (dc2tog) 3 times, dc 9 (24 sts).
Round 17: Dc 10, (dc2tog) 3 times, dc 8 (21 sts).
Round 18: Dc 8, (dc2tog) 3 times, dc 7 (18 sts).
Round 19: Dc 7, (dc2tog) 3 times, dc 5 (15 sts).

Do not stuff past round 19 of the tail. This will make the tail easier to roll and sew in place against the body.

Round 20: Dc 6, (dc2tog) 3 times, dc 3 (12 sts).
Round 21: Dc in each st around (12 sts).
Round 22: (Dc, dc2tog) 4 times (8 sts).
Rounds 23–33: Dc in each st around (8 sts).
Round 34: (Dc, dc2tog, dc) twice (6 sts).

Fasten off and weave the yarn under each of the front loops only, pull tight, and leave a long yarn tail for attaching later.

SPIKES

Using B, work all stitches in a row.
After turning, work back the other way, placing the first st in the 2nd st from the hook.
Row 1: Ch 7, turn (7 sts).
Row 2: Sl st, (dc, ch 2, dc in the same stitch, sl st) 6 times (19 sts).
Fasten off and leave a long tail for attaching later.

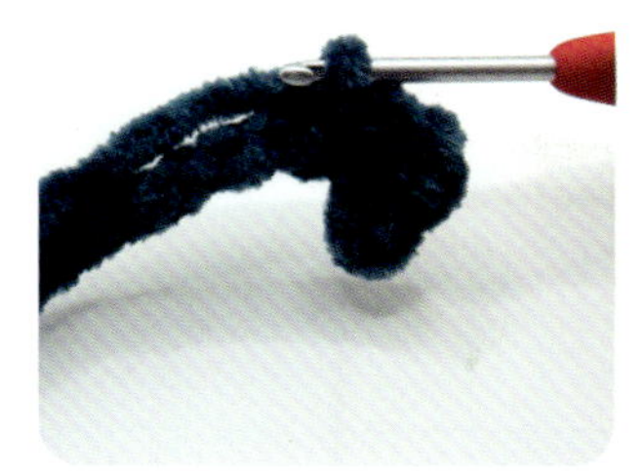

DETAILS AND ASSEMBLY

Tightly roll the tail underneath the body until it reaches round 16. Use a lot of pins to keep it in its place before sewing. With the embroidery needle and the long leftover yarn end from fastening off the tail, whip stitch the pinned tail to the body (see page 18). Bring the needle up through the tail and whip stitch along the tail where the piece meets the underside of the body with 3 to 4 stitches. Make sure the tail is secure, then weave in and hide the yarn end within the body.

Pin the spikes so they are centred on the top portion of the back, beginning between rounds 11 and 12 where the neck curves in. The spikes end between rounds 21 and 22. Whip stitch to attach the spikes, using the embroidery needle and the leftover yarn end. Weave the ends into the body.

Details of how to outline the safety eyes and add the cheeks are on page 19.

FIFI THE FERRET

Many people choose ferrets as family pets because of their undeniable cuteness, adorable faces and slinky bodies. Their curious nature and friendly personalities make them excellent social companions for most families. Crocheting a whimsical Fifi the Ferret will surely add to the entertainment in your home!

Finished size

6in (15cm)

Supplies and materials

- Universal Yarn Bella Chenille, Super Bulky Weight, 100% Polyester, 131yds (120m) per 100g ball
  Yarn A Chocolate 123
  Yarn B Oatmeal 125
  Yarn C Sugar Plum 108
- Hook size: 3.5mm (UK9:USE/4)
- 2 safety eyes ½in (14mm)
- Polyester fibre filling
- Embroidery needle
- Scissors
- Stitch markers
- Sewing pins

Please note: when doing multiple colour changes in a round, you can either cut and tie off the colours after every change or leave a loose running stitch.

FERRET

Using A, work all stitches in a round from bottom to top. Stuff as you crochet.

Round 1: Make a MC with 12 dc (12 sts).
Round 2: (Dc, dc2inc) 6 times (18 sts).
Round 3: (Dc, dc2inc, dc) 6 times (24 sts).
Round 4: (Dc 3, dc2inc) twice, dc, BOB, dc, (dc2inc) twice, dc, BOB, dc, (dc2inc, dc 3) twice (30 sts).
Rounds 5–7: Dc in each st around (30 sts).

The decreases in the next 2 rounds should be between the 2 bobble stitches, if not, adjust the stitches left or right by 1–2 stitches.

Round 8: Dc 12, (dc2tog, dc) twice, dc2tog, dc 10 (27 sts).
Round 9: Dc 9, (dc2tog, dc 2) twice, dc2tog, dc 8 (24 sts).

The bobble stitches in round 11 should line up with the bobble stitches in round 5. If they don't, adjust them left or right by 1–2 stitches.

Round 10: Dc 10, BOB, dc 3, BOB, dc 9 (24 sts).
Round 11: Dc in each st around (24 sts).
Round 12: (Dc, dc2tog, dc) 6 times (18 sts).
Rounds 13–14: Dc in each st around (18 sts).

Fasten off and weave in the yarn ends.
Attach B to the first stitch of round 15.

Round 15: (Dc, dc2inc, dc) 6 times (24 sts).
Round 16: Dc 8, FLO (dc2inc) twice, FLO dc 2, FLO (htr2inc) twice, FLO dc 2, FLO (dc2inc) twice, dc 6 (30 sts).
Round 17: Dc 14, FLO htr, FLO (htr2inc) twice, FLO htr, dc 12 (32 sts).
Round 18: Dc 15, dc2tog, htr 2, dc2tog, dc 11 (30 sts).
Round 19: Dc 9, change to A dc 6, (dc2tog) twice, dc 5, change to B dc 6 (28 sts).

Mark stitches 13 and 20 in round 19. These will be the 2 stitches where you will place the safety eyes later in the pattern.

Round 20: Dc 8, change to A dc 15, change to B dc 5 (28 sts).
Round 21: (Dc 3, dc2tog) twice, dc 4, change to A dc 4, change to B dc 4, dc2tog, dc 2, dc2tog (24 sts).

Add the safety eyes in the marked stitches on round 19. There should be 6 stitches between them.

Round 22: Dc in each st around (24 sts).
Round 23: (Dc, dc2tog, dc) 6 times (18 sts).
Round 24: (Dc, dc2tog) 6 times (12 sts).
Round 25: (Dc, dc2tog) 4 times (8 sts).

Fasten off and weave the yarn under each of the front loops only, pull tight, and hide the end inside the head.

EARS

Inner ear

Make 2 inner ears using A. Work all stitches in a round.
Round 1: Make a MC with 5 dc (5 sts).
Do not close the magic circle but fasten off.

Outer ear

Make 2 outer ears using B. Work all stitches in a round.
Round 1: Make a MC with 5 dc, ch, turn (5 sts).
Do not close the magic circle. Place both the inside and outside parts of the ear together. Make sure both the wrong sides of each piece are facing each other. Dc2inc the next round through both pieces of the ear, making them into one complete ear.
Round 2: (Dc2inc) 5 times (10 sts).
Fasten off and leave a long yarn tail for attaching later.

TAIL

Using A, work all stitches in a round.
Stuff as you crochet.
Round 1: Make a MC with 6 dc (6 sts).
Round 2: Dc in each st around (6 sts).
Round 3: (Dc2inc) 6 times (12 sts).
Rounds 4–6: Dc in each st around (12 sts).
Round 7: (Dc2inc) 3 times, dc 9 (15 sts).
Round 8: Dc 7, (dc2tog) 3 times, dc 2 (12 sts).
Round 9: Dc, (dc2inc) 3 times, dc 8 (15 sts).
Round 10: Dc 8, (dc2tog) 3 times, dc (12 sts).
Round 11: Dc 3, (dc2inc) 3 times, dc 6 (15 sts).
Round 12: Dc 9, (dc2tog) 3 times (12 sts).
Round 13: Dc in each st around (12 sts).
Round 14: Dc 9, htr 3 (12 sts).
Round 15: (Dc, dc2tog) 4 times (8 sts).
Pinch the opening closed. If the seam is not horizontal with the curved tail facing forward, after the last 8 sts, increase or decrease 1–2 stitches.
Dc through both sides with 4 dc and close the opening (4 sts).
Fasten off and leave a long tail for attaching.

DETAILS AND ASSEMBLY

Using pins, mark the width of the nose in the centre of the face between rounds 18 and 19, separated by 3 stitches and about 2 stitches from the safety eyes. Using C, push the embroidery needle through the bottom of the head and out to the first nose pin. Whip stitch a nose at the two pins at least 2–3 times (see page 18). Push the needle back through the same stitch on the bottom of the head and knot the two ends. Weave the ends into the head.

Pin the ears to the side of the top of the head between rounds 19 and 24, approximately 4 stitches from the safety eyes. Make sure the inner ear is facing forwards and that both ears are evenly spaced and centred on the head. Whip stitch them on using the embroidery needle and the leftover yarn ends. Make sure to bring the embroidery needle through both the bottom of the outer and inner ear pieces when whip stitching the centre of the ears. Weave the ends into the head.

Pin the seam of the tail between rounds 4 and 7 on the lower back and centred. Wrap the tail around to the front lower bobble stitch and add a pin to the tip of the tail to keep it in place. This placement is so the tail will help the ferret sit up properly. Once pinned correctly, whip stitch the tail seam to the back with the embroidery needle and the leftover yarn end. Weave the needle through the back to where the 3rd pin is located near the bobble stitch. Add an extra whip stitch or two to keep the tail in place. Weave in the end.

Details of how to outline the safety eyes and add the cheeks are on page 19.

FITZ THE FROG

A frog is an example of a pet that is not cuddly, does not interact with people and is primarily nocturnal. However, our Fitz is a delightful crocheted frog that's all about the cuddles and snuggles without any of the hopping responsibilities of a live pet!

Finished size

3in (7.5cm)

Supplies and materials

- Universal Yarn Bella Chenille, Super Bulky Weight, 100% Polyester, 131yds (120m) per 100g ball
  Yarn A Blueberry 109
  Yarn B Oatmeal 125
- Hook size: 3.5mm (UK9:USE/4)
- 2 safety eyes ¾in (18mm)
- Polyester fibre filling
- Embroidery needle
- Scissors
- Stitch markers
- Sewing pins

Please note: when doing multiple colour changes in a round, you can either cut and tie off the colours after every change or leave a loose running stitch.

FROG

Using A, work all stitches in a round from top to bottom. Stuff as you crochet.
Round 1: Make a MC with 8 dc (8 sts).
Round 2: (Dc2inc) 8 times (16 sts).
Round 3: (Dc, dc2inc) 8 times (24 sts).
Mark stitches 8 and 17 in round 3. These will be the 2 stitches where you will place the safety eyes later in the pattern.
Round 4: Dc 11 (htr2inc) twice, dc 11 (26 sts).
Round 5: Dc 8, change to B BLO dc 3, BLO (dc2tog) twice, BLO dc 3, change to A dc 8 (24 sts).
Round 6: (Dc 3, dc2inc) twice, change to B (dc 3, dc2inc) twice, change to A (dc 3, dc2inc) twice (30 sts).
Add the safety eyes in the marked stitches on round 3. There should be 9 stitches between them.
Rounds 7–10: Dc 10, change to B dc 10, change to A dc 10 (30 sts).
Round 11: Dc2tog, dc 3, dc2tog, dc 2, BOB, change to B (dc 3, dc2tog) twice, change to A BOB, dc 2, dc2tog, dc 3, dc2tog (24 sts).
Cut B and tie off.
Round 12: (Dc, dc2tog, dc) 6 times (18 sts).
Round 13: (Dc, dc2tog) 6 times (12 sts).
Round 14: (Dc, dc2tog) 4 times (8 sts).
Fasten off and weave the yarn under each of the front loops only, pull tight and hide the end inside the head.

EYELIDS

Make 2 eyelids using A. Work all stitches in a row.
Row 1: Ch 6, turn, dc in the 2nd ch from the hook, dc 4 (5 sts).
Fasten off and leave a long yarn tail for attaching later.

ARMS

Make 2 arms using A. Work all stitches in a row. After turning, work the dc stitches down the chains. Do not cut the yarn but repeat this twice to make the 3 connected fingers.

Row 1: Ch 8, turn, dc in the 2nd ch from the hook, dc, sl st, ch 4, turn, dc in the 2nd ch from the hook, dc, sl st, ch 4, turn, dc in the 2nd ch from the hook, dc, sl st, sl st into the starting sl st from the 1st finger, dc 4 down the original starting chain (14 sts).

Fasten off and leave a long yarn tail for attaching later.

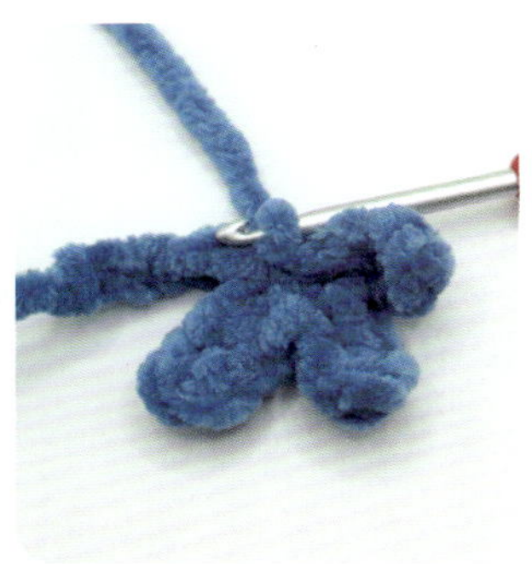

DETAILS AND ASSEMBLY

Flip the frog over and attach A to the 1st front loop only on round 5. Then, sl st across the remaining 10 front loop only stitches on the same round. This creates an upper lip on the frog's face. Fasten off and weave in the ends.

Pin the eyelids to the top of the head, beginning at the inside of the safety eyes and draping down to round 5. They should cover the back portion of the safety eyes. Make sure both the eyelids are evenly spaced on the head. Use the embroidery needle and the leftover yarn end to attach the bottom edge of the eyelid along round 5 with 2 whip stitches (see page 18). Bring the embroidery needle up through to the back of the eyelid and whip stitch along the seam until the end. Weave the ends into the head.

Pin the 2 arms to each side of the frog between rounds 5 and 6, directly below the side of the eyelids. Make sure they are evenly placed. Using the embroidery needle and the leftover yarn ends, whip stitch the back of the arms on to the body with 2 whip stitches. Weave the ends into the body.

Details of how to outline the safety eyes are on page 19.

GALILEO THE GECKO

With over 1,600 species, geckos make great first-time pets. They can grow up to 10in (25cm), live up to 20 years and are docile, which makes them suitable for families. Their habitat should have branches, high-moisture coconut husk substrate, and hiding spots for extra downtime. Galileo the Gecko would especially enjoy some interesting and fun hiding spots to play hide and seek.

Finished size

5½in (14cm)

Supplies and materials

- Universal Yarn Bella Chenille, Super Bulky Weight, 100% Polyester, 131yds (120m) per 100g ball
  Yarn A Boysenberry 124
  Yarn B Amethyst 122
- Hook size: 3.5mm (UK9:USE/4)
- 2 safety eyes ¾in (18mm)
- Polyester fibre filling
- Embroidery needle
- Scissors
- Stitch markers
- Sewing pins

Please note: when doing multiple colour changes in a round, you can either cut and tie off the colours after every change or leave a loose running stitch.

GECKO

Using A, work all stitches in a round from front to back. Stuff as you crochet.

Round 1: Make a MC with 8 dc (8 sts).

Round 2: (Dc, dc2inc) 4 times (12 sts).

Round 3: Dc 3, (dc2inc) 6 times, dc 3 (18 sts).

Round 4: Dc in each st around (18 sts).

Mark stitches 6 and 13 in round 4. These will be the 2 stitches where you place the safety eyes later in the pattern.

Round 5: Dc 4, (dc2inc) 3 times, dc 4, (dc2inc) 3 times, dc 4 (24 sts).

Round 6: Dc in each st around (24 sts).

Round 7: Dc 10, (dc2tog) twice, dc 10 (22 sts).

Place safety eyes on round 4 in the marked stitches, with 6 stitches between them, making sure that the increases in round 5 are centred between each of the safety eyes.

Round 8: Dc 5, (dc2tog) twice, dc 4, (dc2tog) twice, dc 5 (18 sts).

Round 9: Dc in each st around (18 sts).

Round 10: (Dc, dc2inc, dc) 5 times, BOB, dc2inc, dc (24 sts).

The Amethyst stripes between rounds 11–17 should be centred on the back. If they are not, adjust by 1–2 stitches to get the correct placement.

Round 11: Dc 4, BOB, dc 3, (change to B) dc 9, (change to A) dc 7 (24 sts).

Round 12: Dc in each st around (24 sts).

Round 13: Dc 7, (change to B) dc 11, (change to A) dc 6 (24 sts).

Round 14: Dc in each st around (24 sts).

Round 15: Dc 6, (change to B) dc 13, (change to A) dc 2,

BOB, dc 2 (24 sts).
Round 16: Dc 4, BOB, (dc 2, dc2tog) twice, dc, (dc2tog, dc 2) twice, dc 2 (20 sts).
Round 17: Dc 7, (change to B) dc 8, (change to A) dc 5 (20 sts).
Round 18: Dc 7, dc2tog, dc 4, dc2tog, dc 5 (18 sts).
Round 19: (Dc, dc2tog) 6 times (12 sts).
Round 20: (Dc, dc2tog) 4 times (8 sts).
Do not stuff past round 20 of the body. The tail will be unstuffed.
Rounds 21–22: Dc in each st around (8 sts).
Round 23: Dc, sl st 4, dc 3 (8 sts).
Round 24: Dc, FLO sl st 4 only, dc 3 (8 sts).
Rounds 25–26: Dc in each st around (8 sts).
Rounds 27–28: Dc, FLO sl st 4, dc 3 (8 sts).
Rounds 29–30: Dc in each st around (8 sts).
Round 31: (Dc, dc2tog, dc) twice (6 sts).
Rounds 32–35: Dc in each st around (6 sts).
Fasten off and weave the yarn under each of the front loops only, pull tight and hide the end inside the tail.

DETAILS AND ASSEMBLY

Details of how to outline the safety eyes and add the cheeks are on page 19.

HONEY THE HAMSTER

If you're searching for a pet that doesn't require much space but is still furry and soft, a hamster could be the perfect choice. These small rodents are energetic, desk-sized and easy to care for. Our hamster, Honey, doesn't need constant attention but enjoys playtime outside her cage and exploring the rest of the house in a big ball made just for her.

Finished size

5in (12.5cm)

Supplies and materials

- Premier Yarns Parfait Chunky, Super Bulky Weight, 100% Polyester, 131yds (120m) per 100g ball
  Yarn A Mushroom 41
  Yarn B Mustard 29
  Yarn C Cotton Candy 103
- Hook size: 3.5mm (UK9:USE/4)
- 2 safety eyes ½in (14mm)
- Polyester fibre filling
- Embroidery needle
- Scissors
- Stitch markers
- Sewing pins

Please note: when doing multiple colour changes in a round, you can either cut and tie off the colours after every change or leave a loose running stitch.

HAMSTER

Using A, work all stitches in a round from bottom to top. Stuff as you crochet.

Round 1: Make a MC with 12 dc (12 sts).

Round 2: (Dc, dc2inc) 6 times (18 sts).

Round 3: (Dc, dc2inc, dc) 6 times (24 sts).

Change to B for each of the bobble stitches in the next round, then switch to A on the dc stitches.

Round 4: (Dc 3, dc2inc) 4 times, BOB, dc 2, dc2inc, dc, BOB, dc, dc2inc (30 sts).

Rounds 5–7: Dc in each st around (30 sts).

Change to B for each of the bobble stitches in the next round, then switch to A on the dc stitches.

The bobble stitches in round 8 should line up with the bobble stitches in round 4. If they don't, adjust them left or right by 1–2 stitches to get the correct placement.

Round 8: Dc 20, BOB, dc 5, BOB, dc 3 (30 sts).

Round 9: Dc 18, (dc2tog) 6 times (24 sts).

Round 10: (Change to B) Dc 18, (change to A) FLO (dc2inc) 6 times (30 sts).

Rounds 11–12: (Change to B) Dc 18, (change to A) FLO dc 12 (30 sts).

Round 13: (Change to B) Dc 18, (dc2tog) 6 times (24 sts).

Mark stitches 19 and 24 in round 13. These will be the 2 stitches where you will place the safety eyes later in the pattern.

Rounds 14–15: Dc in each st around (24 sts).

Add the safety eyes in the marked stitches on round 13. There should be 4 stitches between them.

Round 16: Dc in each st around (24 sts).

Round 17: (Dc, dc2tog, dc) 6 times (18 sts).

Round 18: (Dc, dc2tog) 6 times (12 sts).

Round 19: (Dc, dc2tog) 4 times (8 sts).

Fasten off and weave the yarn under each of the front loops only, pull tight and hide the end inside the head.

EARS

Make 2 ears using B. Work all stitches in a round.
Round 1: Make a MC with 6 dc (6 sts).
Round 2: (Htr2inc) 6 times (12 sts).
Fasten off and leave a long yarn tail for attaching later.

DETAILS AND ASSEMBLY

Using pins, mark the width of the nose in the centre of the face between rounds 12 and 13, 3 stitches apart. With the embroidery needle and C, push the needle through the side of the head to the first nose pin. Whip stitch a nose at the two pins at least twice (see page 18). Push the needle back through the same stitch on the side of the head. Knot the two ends. Weave the ends into the head.

Pin the ears to the top of the head, 3 stitches away from the safety eyes, with the bottom 3 stitches between rounds 16 and 19. Make sure both the ears are evenly spaced and centred on the head. Whip stitch the ears to the head using the embroidery needle and the leftover yarn end from making the ears. Weave the ends into the head.

Details of how to outline the safety eyes and add the cheeks are on page 19.

LALA THE LLAMA

Llamas are primarily companion animals in farm settings but can make good pets because they are calm and intelligent, requiring less maintenance than some livestock. Their mild temperament and cleanliness make them popular and they can bond with owners and be trained to protect farm areas. Lala, although small in size, is a strong and brave llama who can stand guard in any situation.

Finished size

3½in (9cm)

Supplies and materials

- Universal Yarn Bella Chenille, Super Bulky Weight, 100% Polyester, 131yds (120m) per 100g ball
  Yarn A Blush 127
  Yarn B Sesame 120
  Yarn C Chocolate 123
- Hook size: 3.5mm (UK9:USE/4)
- 2 safety eyes ½in (14mm)
- Polyester fibre filling
- Embroidery needle
- Scissors
- Stitch markers
- Sewing pins

LLAMA

Using A, work all stitches in a round from bottom to top. Stuff as you crochet.

Round 1: Make a MC with 12 dc (12 sts).

Round 2: Dc 3, (dc2inc) 3 times, dc 3, (dc2inc) 3 times (18 sts).

Round 3: Dc 4, (dc2inc, dc) twice, dc2inc, dc 4, (dc2inc, dc) twice, dc2inc (24 sts).

Change to B for each of the bobble stitches in the next round, then switch back to A for all of the dc stitches.

Round 4: Dc 4, dc2inc, (dc, BOB) in the same st, dc2inc, dc 2, dc2inc, (dc, BOB) in the same st, dc2inc, dc 4, dc2inc, (dc, BOB) in the same st, dc2inc, dc 2, dc2inc, (dc, BOB) in the same st, dc2inc (36 sts).

Round 5: Dc in each st around (36 sts).

The bobble stitch in round 6 should be centred between the bobble stitches in round 4. If it is not, adjust it left or right by 1–2 stitches to get the correct placement.

Round 6: Dc 29, BOB, dc 6 (36 sts).

Round 7: Dc in each st around (36 sts).

Round 8: Dc 22, (dc2tog) 3 times, dc 2, (dc2tog) 3 times (30 sts).

Round 9: Dc 21, (dc2tog) twice, dc 3, dc2tog (27 sts).

Round 10: Dc2tog, dc 18, (dc2tog) twice, dc, dc2tog (23 sts).

Round 11: Dc2tog, dc 8, dc2tog, dc 7, dc2tog, dc 2 (20 sts).

Rounds 12–14: Dc in each st around (20 sts).

Round 15: Dc 6, (dc2inc, dc 2) twice, dc2inc, dc 6, dc2inc (24 sts).

Rounds 16–18: Dc in each st around (24 sts).

Mark stitches 9 and 16 in round 18. These will be the 2 stitches where you place the safety eyes later in the pattern.

Round 19: Dc in each st around (24 sts).

Round 20: (Dc, dc2tog, dc) 6 times (18 sts).

Add the safety eyes in the marked stitches on round 18. There should be 6 stitches between them.

Round 21: (Dc, dc2tog) 6 times (12 sts).

Round 22: (Dc, dc2tog) 4 times (8 sts).

Fasten off and weave the yarn under each of the front loops only, pull tight and hide the end inside the head.

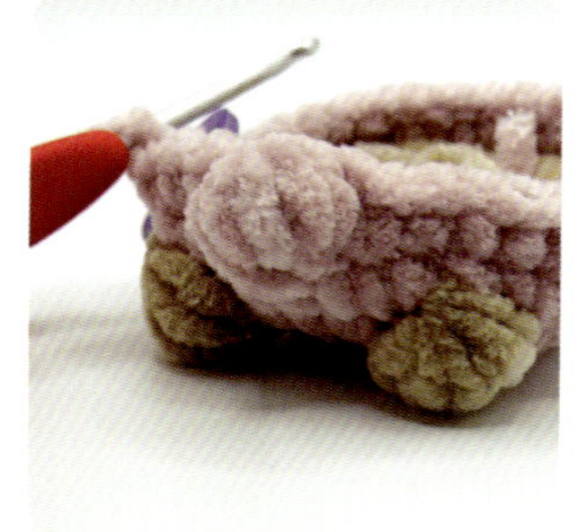

EARS

Make 2 ears using A. Work all stitches in a round.

Round 1: Make a MC with 6 dc, ch, turn (6 sts).

Round 2: (Dc2inc) 6 times, ch, turn (12 sts).

Round 3: Dc 2, htr 2, htr2inc, (tr2inc) twice, htr2inc htr 2, dc 2, ch (16 sts).

Pinch the ear closed and dc across with 4 stitches connecting both sides, closing the bottom of the ear and creating a small seam.

Fasten off and leave a long yarn tail for attaching later.

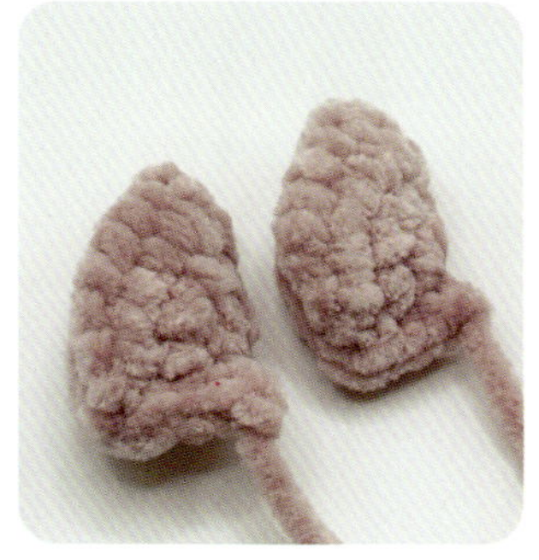

MUZZLE

Using B, work all stitches in a round.

Round 1: Make a MC with 6 dc (6 sts).

Round 2: (Dc2inc) 6 times (12 sts).

Round 3: Dc in each st around (12 sts).

Fasten off and leave a long yarn tail for attaching later.

DETAILS AND ASSEMBLY

Using 3 pins, mark a V-shaped nose on the centre of the muzzle between the magic circle and rounds 1 and 2. With the embroidery needle and C, push the yarn through the bottom of the muzzle and out at the lower nose pin. Add one whip stitch up to one of the top pins (see page 18), bring the needle horizontally through the nose to the second top pin and out. Sew the last whip stitch down through the lower pin spot where you first entered to complete the V shape. Push the yarn back through the same stitch on the bottom of the muzzle, knot the two ends, and weave the ends into the head.

Pin the muzzle to the front of the face between the safety eyes. The top of the muzzle should be between rounds 18 and 19 and the bottom between rounds 13 and 14. Make sure it is centred on the face. Whip stitch it on using the embroidery needle and the leftover yarn end. Start at the bottom of the muzzle and work around in a circle. Before closing the last 4 whip stitches, lightly stuff the muzzle to ensure it keeps its shape. Weave the ends into the head.

Pin the ears to the side of the head with the seam between rounds 19 and 20, and 2 stitches past the safety eyes. Make sure both the ears are evenly spaced on the head and facing forwards. Whip stitch them on using the embroidery needle and the leftover yarn end from attaching the two ear pieces together. Sew along the seam, then bring the needle up through the head to the back of the ear near the seam. Add a whip stitch to the back edge of the ear to secure it to the top of the head and prevent it from flopping over. Weave the ends into the head.

Details of how to outline the safety eyes and add the cheeks are on page 19.

LUCKY THE LOP BUNNY

Lop bunnies are a distinctive breed of rabbit, easily recognized by their long, floppy ears and gentle nature. While they may be a bit shy at first, they typically become relaxed and affectionate once they feel comfortable. A lop bunny like Lucky makes a lovable companion – soft, furry and full of sweet charm.

Finished size

4in (10cm)

Supplies and materials

- Universal Yarn Bella Chenille, Super Bulky Weight, 100% Polyester, 131yds (120m) per 100g ball
  Yarn A Snowy 101
  Yarn B Elephant 118
  Yarn C Sugar Plum 108
- Hook size: 3.5mm (UK9:USE/4)
- 2 safety eyes ½in (14mm)
- Polyester fibre filling
- Embroidery needle
- Scissors
- Stitch markers
- Sewing pins

Please note: when doing multiple colour changes in a round, you can either cut and tie off the colours after every change or leave a loose running stitch.

LOP BUNNY

Using A, work all stitches in a round from bottom to top. Stuff as you crochet.

Round 1: Make a MC with 12 dc (12 sts).
Round 2: (Dc, dc2inc) 6 times (18 sts).
Round 3: (Dc, dc2inc, dc) 6 times (24 sts).
Round 4: (Dc 3, dc2inc) twice, dc, BOB, dc, (dc2inc) twice, dc, BOB, dc, (dc2inc, dc 3) twice (30 sts).
Round 5: Dc in each st around (30 sts).

The BOB stitch on round 6 should be centred on the back. If it isn't, adjust it left or right by 1–2 stitches.

Round 6: BOB, dc 29 (30 sts).
Round 7: Dc in each st around (30 sts).

The bobble stitches in the next round should be directly above the bobble stitches in round 4. If not, increase or decrease 1–2 stitches.

Round 8: Dc 11, BOB, dc 6, BOB, dc 11 (30 sts).
Round 9: Dc 9, (dc2tog) 6 times, dc 9 (24 sts).
Round 10: Dc 7, FLO (dc2inc) 10 times only, dc 7 (34 sts).
Round 11: Dc in each st around (34 sts).
Round 12: Dc 13, change to B dc 2, change to A dc 4, change to B dc 2, change to A dc 13 (34 sts).
Round 13: Dc 10, change to B dc, (dc2tog) 6 times, dc, change to A dc 10 (28 sts).

Mark stitches 12 and 18 in round 13. These will be the 2 stitches where you will place the safety eyes later in the pattern.

Round 14: Dc 9, change to B dc 10, change to A dc 9 (28 sts).
Round 15: Dc 5, dc2tog, dc, change to B dc 4, dc2tog, dc 5, dc2tog, change to A dc 5, dc2tog (24 sts).

Add the safety eyes in the marked stitches on round 13. There should be 5 stitches between them.

Round 16: Dc 10, change to B dc 5, change to A dc 9 (24 sts).
Round 17: (Dc, dc2tog, dc) twice, dc, change to B dc2tog, (dc 2, dc2tog) 3 times, dc (18 sts).
Round 18: (Dc, dc2tog) 6 times (12 sts).
Round 19: (Dc, dc2tog) 4 times (8 sts).

Fasten off and weave the yarn under each of the front loops only, pull tight and hide the end inside the head.

EARS

Make 2 ears using B. Work all stitches in a round. Do not stuff.

Round 1: Make a MC with 6 dc (6 sts).
Round 2: (Dc2inc) 6 times (12 sts).
Round 3: (Dc, dc2inc) 6 times (18 sts).
Round 4: Dc in each st around (18 sts).
Round 5: (Dc, dc2inc, dc) 6 times (24 sts).
Round 6-8: Dc in each st around (24 sts).
Round 9: (Dc, dc2tog, dc) 6 times (18 sts).
Round 10-11: Dc in each st around (18 sts).
Round 12: (Dc, dc2tog) 6 times (12 sts).
Round 13-14: Dc in each st around (12 sts).

Pinch the opening closed, dc through both sides with 6 dc and close the opening (6 sts).
Fasten off and leave a long yarn tail for attaching later.

DETAILS AND ASSEMBLY

Using 3 pins, mark a V-shaped nose between rounds 12 and 13, 4 stitches apart. With the embroidery needle and C, push the yarn through the bottom of the head and out at the lower nose pin. Add one whip stitch up to one of the top pins, bring the needle horizontally through the nose to the second top pin and out. Sew the last whip stitch through the lower pin spot to complete the V shape. Push the yarn back through the same stitch on the bottom of the head, knot the two ends and weave the ends into the head.

Pin the ears to the side of the head with the seam between rounds 14 and 15, 2 stitches past the safety eyes. Make sure both the ears are evenly spaced on the head. Whip stitch them on, sewing along the seam using the embroidery needle and the leftover yarn end. Weave the ends into the head.

Details of how to outline the safety eyes and add the cheeks are on page 19.

SMOKEY THE SCOTTISH FOLD

Scottish folds are known for their distinctive small, folded ears, round faces and incredibly soft paws. These cats are affectionate, friendly, calm, social, curious and intelligent. Smokey's charming appearance and gentle personality will shine through in any colour yarn you choose.

Finished size

5in (12.5cm)

Supplies and materials

- Premier Yarns Parfait Chunky, Super Bulky Weight, 100% Polyester, 131yds (120m) per 100g ball
  Yarn A Light Blue 05
  Yarn B White 01
  Yarn C Cotton Candy 03
- Hook size: 3.5mm (UK9:USE/4)
- 2 safety eyes ½in (14mm)
- Polyester fibre filling
- Embroidery needle
- Scissors
- Stitch markers
- Sewing pins

Please note: when doing multiple colour changes in a round, you can either cut and tie off the colours after every change or leave a loose running stitch.

SCOTTISH FOLD

Using A, work all stitches in a round from bottom to top. Stuff as you crochet.

Round 1: Make a MC with 12 dc (12 sts).
Round 2: (Dc, dc2inc) 6 times (18 sts).
Round 3: (Dc, dc2inc, dc) 6 times (24 sts).
Round 4: Dc 3, dc2inc, dc, BOB, dc, dc2inc, dc, change to B BOB, dc, (dc2inc) twice, dc, BOB, dc, change to A dc2inc, dc, BOB, dc, dc2inc, dc 3 (30 sts).
Rounds 5–8: Dc 11, change to B dc 9, change to A dc 10 (30 sts).
Round 9: (Dc 3, dc2tog) twice, dc, change to B dc 2, dc2tog, dc 3, dc2tog, change to A (dc 3, dc2tog) twice (24 sts).
All the stitches in round 10 need to be worked in the FLO.
Round 10: FLO (dc 3, dc2inc) twice, dc, change to B dc 2, dc2inc, dc 3, dc2inc, change to A (dc 3, dc2inc) twice (30 sts).
Round 11: Dc 11, change to B FLO dc 9, change to A dc 10 (30 sts)
Round 12: Dc 11, change to B dc 3, BOB, dc, BOB, dc 3, change to A dc 10 (30 sts).
Mark stitches 14 and 19 in round 13. These will be the 2 stitches where you will place the safety eyes later in the pattern.
Round 13: Dc 14, change to B dc 3, change to A dc 13 (30 sts).
The single dc stitch in B in round 14 should be centred between the 2 BOB stitches from round 12. If it is not, please adjust it right or left by 1 stitch.
Round 14: Dc 15, change to B dc, change to A dc 14 (30 sts).
Round 15: Dc in each st around (30 sts).
Add the safety eyes in the marked stitches on round 13. There should be 4 stitches between them.
Round 16: (Dc 3, dc2tog) 6 times (24 sts).
Round 17: (Dc, dc2tog, dc) 6 times (18 sts).
Round 18: (Dc, dc2tog) 6 times (12 sts).
Round 19: (Dc, dc2tog) 4 times (8 sts).
Fasten off and weave the yarn under each of the FLO, pull tight and hide the end inside the head.

TAIL

Using A, work all stitches in a round.
Stuff as you crochet.
Round 1: Make a MC with 12 dc (12 sts).
Rounds 2–6: Dc in each st around (12 sts).
Round 7: (Dc, dc2tog) 4 times (8 sts).
Rounds 8–10: Dc in each st around (8 sts).
Pinch the opening closed, dc through both sides with 4 dc and close the opening (4 sts).
Fasten off and leave a long yarn tail for attaching later.

EARS

Make 2 ears using A. Work all stitches in a row.
When turning, put the stitch in the 2nd ch from the hook.
Row 1: Start with a long yarn tail approximately 6in (15cm), ch 5, turn (5 sts).
Row 2: Dc in each st across, ch, turn (4 sts).
Row 3: (Dc2tog) twice, ch, turn (2 sts).
Row 4: Dc2tog, ch, turn (1 st).
Turn and work a dc2inc in the last decrease then dc 3 along the first side of the ear, dc2inc in the corner, dc 2 along the bottom of the ear, dc2inc in the 3rd corner, then work dc 3 up the last side of the ear. Fasten off and weave the yarn end down through the bottom of the ear (approx. 14 sts).
The starting yarn tail is for attaching the ears later.

DETAILS AND ASSEMBLY

With the embroidery needle and C, push the yarn through the side of the head and out at the White stitch between the BOB stitches on the face. Add about 6 whip stitches around that centred stitch until the nose is a little puffy. Bring the needle back through the same stitch on the side of the head, knot the two ends and weave the ends into the head.

Pin the ears to the top of the head with the bottom seam between rounds 15 and 19, 1–2 stitches apart. The bottom seam of the ears should be 5–6 stitches past the safety eyes. Make sure both the ears are evenly spaced on the head. Whip stitch them on, sewing along the seam with the embroidery needle and the starting yarn end. Make sure to push the ears down flat against the top of the head. Weave the ends into the head.

Pin the tail between rounds 4 and 7 on the lower back, centred but at an angle so the tail is not directly behind the cat's body. Once pinned correctly, use the embroidery needle and the long yarn tail to whip stitch the tail on. Weave the needle through the back, 2–3 rounds up, and add an extra whip stitch or two to the tail to keep it in place. Weave in the end.

Details of how to outline the safety eyes and add the cheeks are on page 19.

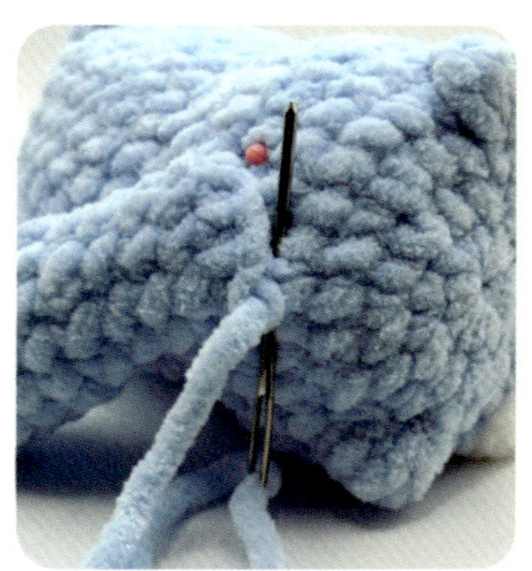

PEEWEE THE POODLE

Poodles are available in three sizes: toy poodles, miniature poodles and standard poodles. They have a curly, hypoallergenic coat and typically live between 10 to 18 years. Poodles are known for their minimal health issues and are recognized as intelligent, affectionate and active dog breeds. A crocheted poodle like Peewee would be a tiny, toy-sized dog, making her the smallest poodle around.

Finished size

6in (15cm)

Supplies and materials

- Premier Yarns Parfait Chunky, Super Bulky Weight, 100% Polyester, 131yds (120m) per 100g ball
  Yarn A Pale Gray 24
  Yarn B White 01
  Yarn C Black 10
- Hook size: 3.5mm (UK9:USE/4)
- 2 safety eyes ½in (14mm)
- Polyester fibre filling
- Embroidery needle
- Scissors
- Stitch markers
- Sewing pins
- Poly pellets (optional)

Please note: when doing multiple colour changes in a round, you can either cut and tie off the colours after every change or leave a loose running stitch.

POODLE

Using A, work all stitches in a round from back to front. Stuff as you crochet and add poly pellets when instructed (see page 9).

Round 1: Make a MC with 12 dc (12 sts).

Round 2: (Dc, dc2inc) 6 times (18 sts).

Round 3: (Dc, dc2inc, dc) 6 times (24 sts).

Change to B for each of the BOB stitches in the next 3 rounds, then switch back to A for the dc stitches.

Round 4: (Dc 3, dc2inc) 3 times, BOB, dc 2, dc2inc, (dc 3, dc2inc) 2 times (30 sts).

Round 5: Dc 27, BOB, dc 2 (30 sts).

Round 6: Dc 3, BOB, dc 26 (30 sts).

Rounds 7–9: Dc in each st around (30 sts).

Round 10: Dc 28, BOB, dc (30 sts).

Round 11: Dc 4, BOB, dc 25 (30 sts).

Optional: Add a small stocking with poly pellets to weight down the back end of the dog. Continue to stuff as you crochet.

Round 12: (Dc2tog) twice, dc 2, (dc2tog) twice, dc 4, (dc2inc, dc) twice, dc2inc, dc 4, (dc2tog) twice, dc 3 (27 sts).

Round 13: (Dc2tog, dc) twice, dc2tog, dc 2, (dc2inc, dc) 4 times, dc2inc, dc 2, (dc2tog, dc) twice (27 sts).

Round 14: Dc in each st around (27 sts).

Round 15: (Dc2tog) twice, dc 6, (dc2inc, dc 2) 3 times, dc2inc, dc 5, dc2tog (28 sts).

Round 16: Dc 10, change to B (dc 2, BOB) twice, dc 2, change to A dc 10 (28 sts).

Round 17: (Dc2inc) twice, dc 3, change to B dc 6, (BOB, dc 2) twice, BOB, dc 6, change to A dc 2, (dc2inc) twice (32 sts).

Round 18: Dc 7, change to B (dc, dc2tog, dc) twice, BOB, dc 2, BOB, (dc, dc2tog, dc) twice, change to A dc 5 (28 sts).

Round 19: Dc 5, dc2tog, change to B (dc 5, dc2tog), twice, dc 2, change to A dc 3, dc2tog (24 sts).

Mark stitches 11 and 18 in round 20. These will be the 2 stitches where you will place the safety eyes later in the pattern.

Round 20: Dc in each st around (24 sts).

Round 21: Dc 8, (dc2tog, dc) 3 times, dc2tog, dc 5 (20 sts).

Round 22: Dc in each st around (20 sts).

Add the safety eyes in the marked stitches on round 20. There should be 6 stitches between them.

Round 23: (Dc, dc2tog) 3 times, dc 5, (dc2tog, dc) twice (15 sts).

Round 24: (Dc2tog) twice, dc 9, dc2tog (12 sts).

Round 25: (Dc, dc2tog) 4 times (8 sts).

Fasten off and weave the yarn under each of the FLO, pull tight and hide the end inside the head.

EARS

Make 2 ears using B. Work all stitches in a round from bottom to top.
Do not stuff.
Round 1: Make a MC with 12 dc (12 sts).
Round 2: (Dc, dc2inc) 6 times (18 sts).
Round 3: (Dc 2, BOB) 6 times (18 sts).
Round 4: Dc in each st around (18 sts).
Round 5: (Dc, BOB, dc) 6 times (18 sts).
Round 6: Dc in each st around (18 sts).
Round 7: (BOB, dc 2) 6 times (18 sts).
Round 8: Dc in each st around (18 sts).
Round 9: (Dc, dc2tog) 6 times (12 sts).
Round 10: Dc in each st around (12 sts).
Pinch the opening closed, dc through both sides with 6 dc and close the opening (6 sts).
Fasten off and leave a long yarn tail for attaching later.

DETAILS AND ASSEMBLY

Using pins, mark the width of the nose in the centre of the face between rounds 24 and 25 and 3 stitches apart. With the embroidery needle and C, push the yarn through the side of the head to the first nose pin. Whip stitch at least 3 stitches between the two pins to make the nose. Push the yarn back through the same stitch on the side of the head and knot the two ends. Weave the ends into the head.

Pin the ears to the side of the head between rounds 17 and 14 underneath the BOB stitch on round 17, reaching up to the BOB stitch on round 15. The ears should be pinned diagnally along the 2 BOB stitches. Make sure the ears are evenly spaced. Whip stitch them on using the embroidery needle and the yarn end from closing the ears. Weave the ends into the head.

Details of how to outline the safety eyes and add the cheeks are on page 19.

GOLDIE THE GOLDFISH

Goldfish are social animals and make great pets, especially for individuals highly allergic to other types of pets. As social creatures, they thrive on companionship and may even eat from their owner's hand. Who wouldn't want a cheerful little fish like Goldie the Goldfish, who brings a splash of colour to your life while being an allergy-friendly companion that won't make you sneeze!

Finished size

4in (10cm)

Supplies and materials

- Universal Yarn Bella Chenille, Super Bulky Weight, 100% Polyester, 131yds (120m) per 100g ball
  Yarn A Peach 115
  Yarn B Apricot 129
  Yarn C Bright Salmon 106
- Hook size: 3.5mm (UK9:USE/4)
- 2 safety eyes ½in (14mm)
- Polyester fibre filling
- Embroidery needle
- Scissors
- Stitch markers
- Sewing pins

GOLDFISH

Using A, work all stitches in a round from front to back. Stuff as you crochet.

Round 1: Make a MC with 6 dc (6 sts).
Round 2: Dc in each st around (6 sts).
Round 3: (Dc, dc2inc) 3 times (9 sts).
Round 4: (Dc2inc) 9 times (18 sts).
Round 5: Dc in each st around (18 sts).
Round 6: (Dc, dc2inc, dc) 6 times (24 sts).
Mark stitches 6 and 17 in round 6. These will be the 2 stitches where you place the safety eyes later in the pattern.
Rounds 7–8: Dc in each st around (24 sts).
Place safety eyes on round 6 in the marked stitches, with 10 stitches between them.
Change to B on the last stitch of round 8. Cut A and tie off.
Round 9: Dc in each st around (24 sts).
Round 10: (Dc, dc2tog, dc) 6 times (18 sts).
Round 11: Dc in each st around (18 sts).
Round 12: (Dc, dc2tog) 6 times (12 sts).
Pinch the opening closed, if the seam is not centred with the middle of the safety eyes, increase or decrease 1–2 stitches.
Crochet 6 dc through both sides to close up the opening, change to C and ch 2, turn (6 sts).
Cut B and tie off.

TAIL

Row 1: Tr2inc into dc, tr 4, tr2inc, ch 2, sl st to the same stitch as the last tr (8 sts).
Fasten off and weave in the yarn ends.

TOP FIN

Using C, work all stitches in a row.
After turning, work back the other way, placing the first st in the 2nd st from the hook.

Row 1: Ch 5, turn (5 sts).

Row 2: Tr2inc, htr 2, tr, ch 2, sl st to the same stitch as the last tr (5 sts).

Fasten off and leave a long yarn tail for attaching later.

SIDE FINS

Make 2 using C. Work all stitches in a row.
After each row, turn and work back the other way, placing the first st in the 2nd st from the hook.

Row 1: Ch 4, turn (4 sts).

Row 2: Htr (tr, ch 2, sl st in the 2nd ch from hook, tr) in the next stitch, htr (4 sts).

Fasten off and leave a long yarn tail for attaching later.

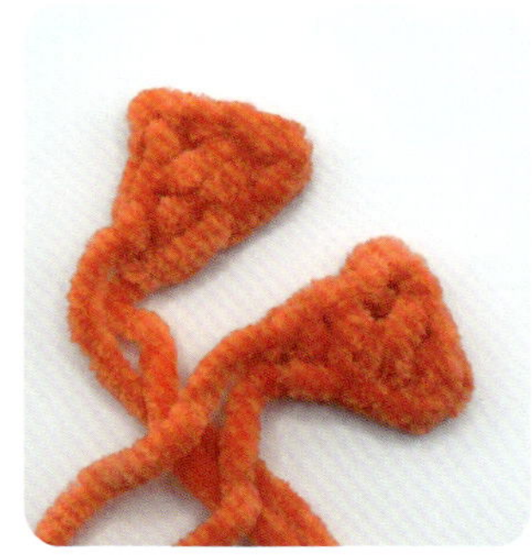

DETAILS AND ASSEMBLY

Pin the bottom fins to the underside of the body starting between rounds 5 and 6, 3 rounds below the start of the safety eyes. They should have the points facing down, like an upside-down triangle. Make sure the fins are evenly spaced with 3 stitches between them. Flip the fish upside down and whip stitch the fins on using the embroidery needle and the leftover yarn ends (see page 18). Weave the ends into the body.

Pin the top fin to the fish beginning between rounds 6 and 7, directly above the middle of the safety eyes, and ending between rounds 10 and 11, a round before the tail. When centred on the top of the fish body, whip stitch it on, using the embroidery needle and the leftover yarn ends. Weave the ends into the body.

Details of how to outline the safety eyes and add the cheeks are on page 19.

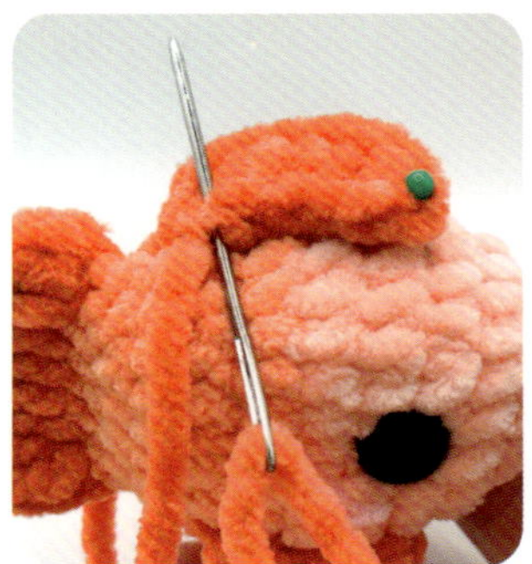

GATSBY THE GUINEA PIG

Guinea pigs are actually rodents, not pigs! They typically sleep only a few hours, which makes it easy and enjoyable to play and socialize with them. While they are generally quiet, they can become quite vocal when excited, making adorable sounds such as squeaks and even purrs. So, if you were to crochet two or more charming little guinea pigs, you would end up with a delightful squeaking herd.

Finished size

5in (12.5cm)

Supplies and materials

- Universal Yarn Bella Chenille, Super Bulky Weight, 100% Polyester, 131yds (120m) per 100g ball
  Yarn A Chocolate 123
  Yarn B Sesame 120
  Yarn C Oatmeal 125
  Yarn D Blush 127
- Hook size: 3.5mm (UK9:USE/4)
- 2 safety eyes ½in (14mm)
- Polyester fibre filling
- Embroidery needle
- Scissors
- Stitch markers
- Sewing pins

Please note: when doing multiple colour changes in a round, you can either cut and tie off the colours after every change or leave a loose running stitch.

GUINEA PIG

Using A, work all stitches in a round from bottom to top. Stuff as you crochet.

Round 1: Make a MC with 12 dc (12 sts).
Round 2: (Dc, dc2inc) 6 times (18 sts).
Round 3: (Dc, dc2inc, dc) 6 times (24 sts).
Round 4: (Dc 3, dc2inc) 6 times (30 sts).
Round 5: Dc in each st around (30 sts).
Round 6: Dc 22, BOB, dc 5, BOB, dc (30 sts).
Change to B on the last stitch of round 6.
Round 7: Dc in each st around (30 sts).
Round 8: (Dc 3, dc2tog) 6 times (24 sts).
Round 9: Dc in each st around (24 sts).
Round 10: Dc 19, BOB, dc 3, BOB (24 sts).
Change to A on the last stitch of round 10.
Rounds 11–13: Dc in each st around (24 sts).
Change to C on the last stitch of round 13.
Cut off A and tie off.
Round 14: (Dc, dc2tog, dc) 6 times (18 sts).
Round 15: Dc in each st around (18 sts).
Round 16: Dc 2, change to A dc 4, change to C dc 3, change to A dc 4, change to C dc 5 (18 sts).
Mark stitches 5 and 11 in round 16. These will be the 2 stitches where you will place the safety eyes later in the pattern.
Round 17: Dc 2, change to A dc 4, change to C dc 3, change to A dc 4, change to C dc 5 (18 sts).
Cut A and tie off.
Round 18: Dc in each st around (18 sts).
Add the safety eyes in the marked stitches on round 16. There should be 5 stitches between them, and they should be near the centre of the Chocolate-coloured stripes.
Round 19: (Dc, dc2tog) 6 times (12 sts).
Round 20: (Dc, dc2tog) 4 times (8 sts).
Fasten off and weave in the yarn ends.

EARS

Using A and B, work all stitches in a round.
Make 2 ears, one in each colour.
Round 1: Make a MC with 8 dc, ch, turn (8 sts).
Round 2: Dc in each st around (8 sts).
Do not close the round but fasten off and leave a long yarn tail for attaching later.

DETAILS AND ASSEMBLY

Using pins, mark the width of the nose in the centre of the face between rounds 18 and 19, 2 stitches apart. With the embroidery needle, push yarn D through the bottom of the head to the first nose pin. Whip stitch a nose at the two pins at least twice (see page 18). Push the yarn back through the same stitch on the bottom of the head and knot the two ends. Weave the ends into the head.

Pin the ears to the top of the head between rounds 13 and 14 with 2 stitches separating them. Make sure both the ears are evenly spaced on the head and lined up with the safety eyes. Whip stitch the bottom portion of the ears on to the head using the embroidery needle and the leftover yarn end. Weave the ends into the head.

Details of how to outline the safety eyes and add the cheeks are on page 19.

CHEDDAR THE CORGI

The corgi is one of the most charming herding dog breeds. They are irresistibly cute, with short, stubby legs, expressive faces and dirt-repellent coats. These high-energy, intelligent dogs are quick learners, making them easy to train. Cheddar can be a wonderful family pet with his stubby legs and adorable face, making him absolutely irresistible.

Finished size

6in (15cm)

Supplies and materials

- Premier Yarns Parfait Chunky, Super Bulky Weight, 100% Polyester, 131yds (120m) per 100g ball
  Yarn A Tangerine 15
  Yarn B Cream 07
  Yarn C Chocolate 35
- Hook size: 3.5mm (UK9:USE/4)
- 2 safety eyes ½in (14mm)
- Polyester fibre filling
- Embroidery needle
- Scissors
- Stitch markers
- Sewing pins
- Poly pellets (optional)

Please note: when doing multiple colour changes in a round, you can either cut and tie off the colours after every change or leave a loose running stitch.

CORGI

Using A, work all stitches in a round from back to front. Stuff as you crochet and add poly pellets when instructed (see page 9).

Round 1: Make a MC with 12 dc (12 sts).
Round 2: (Dc, dc2inc) 6 times (18 sts).
Round 3: (Dc, dc2inc, dc) 6 times (24 sts).
Round 4: (Dc 3, dc2inc) 3 times, BOB, dc 2, dc2inc, (dc 3, dc2inc) 2 times (30 sts).
Round 5: Dc 27, BOB, dc 2 (30 sts).
Round 6: Dc 3, BOB, dc 26 (30 sts).
Rounds 7–8: Dc in each st around (30 sts).
Change to B on the last stitch of round 8.
Round 9: Dc in each st around (30 sts).
Round 10: Dc 28, BOB, dc (30 sts).
Round 11: Dc 4, BOB, dc 25 (30 sts).
Optional: Add a small stocking with poly pellets to weight down the back end of the dog. Continue to stuff as you crochet.
Round 12: (Dc2tog) twice, dc 2, (dc2tog) twice, dc 5, dc2inc, dc 2, dc2inc, dc 5, (dc2tog) twice, dc 2 (26 sts).
Round 13: (Dc2tog, dc) twice, dc2tog, dc 2, (dc2inc, dc) 4 times, dc2inc, dc 2, dc2tog, dc, dc2tog (26 sts).
Round 14: Dc in each st around (26 sts).
Round 15: (Dc2tog) twice, dc 4, change to A dc, (dc2inc, dc 2) 3 times, dc2inc, dc, change to B dc 4, dc2tog (27 sts).
Round 16: Dc 6 change to A dc 17, change to B dc 4 (27 sts).
Round 17: (Dc2inc) 3 times, dc 3, change to A dc 17, change to B dc 2, (dc2inc) twice (32 sts).
Round 18: Dc 9, change to A dc, (dc2tog, dc 2) 3 times, dc2tog, dc 2, change to B dc 6 (28 sts).
Round 19: Dc 5, dc2tog, dc 2, change to A dc 2, dc2tog, dc, change to B dc 3, change to A dc, dc2tog, dc 2, change to B dc 3, dc2tog, dc (24 sts).
Mark stitches 11 and 18 in round 20. These will be the 2 stitches where you will place the safety eyes later in the pattern.
Round 20: Dc 8, change to A dc 4, change to B dc 3, change to A dc 4, change to B dc 5 (24 sts).
Round 21: Dc 8, change to A dc, dc2tog, dc, change to B dc2tog, dc, change to A dc2tog, dc, dc2tog, change to B dc 4 (20 sts).
Round 22: Dc in each st around (20 sts).
Add the safety eyes in the marked stitches on round 20. There should be 6 stitches between them, with the 3 Cream stitches centred between each of the safety eyes. If not, adjust them 1–2 stitches left or right to get the correct placement.
Round 23: Dc 2, (dc2tog, dc) twice, dc2tog, dc 5, dc2tog, dc, dc2tog (15 sts).
Round 24: (Dc2tog) twice dc 9, dc2tog (12 sts).
Round 25: (Dc, dc2tog) 4 times (8 sts).
Fasten off and weave the yarn under each of the FLO, pull tight and hide the end inside the head.

EARS

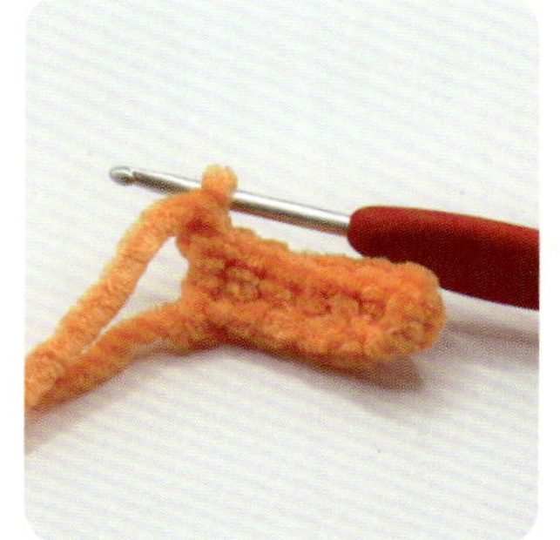

Make 2 ears using A. Work all stitches in a row. When turning, put the first stitch in the 2nd ch from the hook.

Row 1: Start with a long yarn tail approximately 6in (15cm), ch 7, turn (7 sts).

Row 2: Dc in each st across, ch turn (6 sts).

Row 3: Dc2tog, dc 2, dc2tog, ch, turn (4 sts).

Row 4: Dc in each st across, ch turn (4 sts).

Row 5: (Dc2tog) twice, ch, turn (2 sts).

Row 6: Dc in each st across, ch turn (2 sts).

Row 7: Dc2tog, ch turn (1 st).

Turn and work approximately 6–7 dc along the 2 long sides and 4 dc sts along the bottom of the ear, placing dc2inc in each of the 3 corners. Fasten off and weave in the yarn end (approx. 24 sts).

The starting yarn tail is for attaching the ears later.

DETAILS AND ASSEMBLY

Pin the ears to the top of the head between rounds 15 and 16 with 3 stitches separating them. Make sure the ears are evenly spaced on the head and lined up with the safety eyes. The outside bottom of each ear should end near the colour change on each side of the head. Whip stitch them on using the embroidery needle and the yarn end from starting the ears. Weave the ends into the head.

Using pins, mark the width of the nose in the centre of the face between rounds 24 and 25 and 3 stitches apart. With the embroidery needle and C, push the needle through the side of the head to the first nose pin. Whip stitch at least 3 stitches between the pins to make the nose.

Push the yarn back through the first stitch on the side of the head and knot the two ends. Weave the ends into the head.

Details of how to outline the safety eyes and add the cheeks are on page 19.

MOZART THE MOUSE

Mice are amusing, pocket-sized pets that are extremely social, intelligent creatures, and when kept in pairs, they can communicate using ultrasonic sounds that humans cannot hear. Mice are quiet and do not require constant attention, making them low-maintenance pets. While they may not enjoy being held, Mozart the Mouse does. He makes a great first-time and entertaining pet.

Finished size

5in (12.5cm)

Supplies and materials

- Universal Yarn Bella Chenille, Super Bulky Weight, 100% Polyester, 131yds (120m) per 100g ball
  Yarn A Snowy 101
  Yarn B Blush 127
  Yarn C Sugar Plum 108
- Hook size: 3.5mm (UK9:USE/4)
- 2 safety eyes ½in (14mm)
- Polyester fibre filling
- Embroidery needle
- Scissors
- Stitch markers
- Sewing pins

MOUSE

Using A, work all stitches in a round from bottom to top. Stuff as you crochet.

Round 1: Make a MC with 12 dc (12 sts).
Round 2: (Dc, dc2inc) 6 times (18 sts).
Round 3: (Dc, dc2inc, dc) 6 times (24 sts).
Round 4: (Dc 3, dc2inc) 6 times (30 sts).
Round 5: Dc in each st around (30 sts).
Change to B for each of the bobble stitches in the next round, then switch back to A for all of the dc stitches.
Round 6: Dc 2, BOB, dc 5, BOB, dc 21 (30 sts).
Round 7: Dc in each st around (30 sts).
Round 8: (Dc 3, dc2tog) 6 times (24 sts).
Round 9: Dc in each st around (24 sts).
Change to B for each of the bobble stitches in the next round, then switch back to A for all of the dc stitches.
Round 10: Dc 3, BOB, dc 2, BOB, dc 17 (24 sts).
Rounds 11–13: Dc in each st around (24 sts).
Mark stitches 15 and 22 in round 13. These will be the 2 stitches where you place the safety eyes later in the pattern.
Round 14: (Dc, dc2tog, dc) 6 times (18 sts).
Round 15: Dc in each st around (18 sts).
Add the safety eyes in the marked stitches on round 13. There should be 7 stitches between them. If the safety eyes are not even or spaced correctly with the last bobble stitches (feet), adjust by 1–2 stitches to the right or left.
Round 16: (Dc, dc2tog) 6 times (12 sts).
Round 17: (Dc, dc2tog) 4 times (8 sts).
Fasten off and weave the yarn under each of the front loops only, pull tight and hide the end inside the head.

EARS

Make 2 ears using B. Work all stitches in a round.
Round 1: Make a MC with 6 dc (6 sts).
Round 2: (Dc2inc) 6 times (12 sts).
Fasten off and leave a long yarn tail for attaching later.

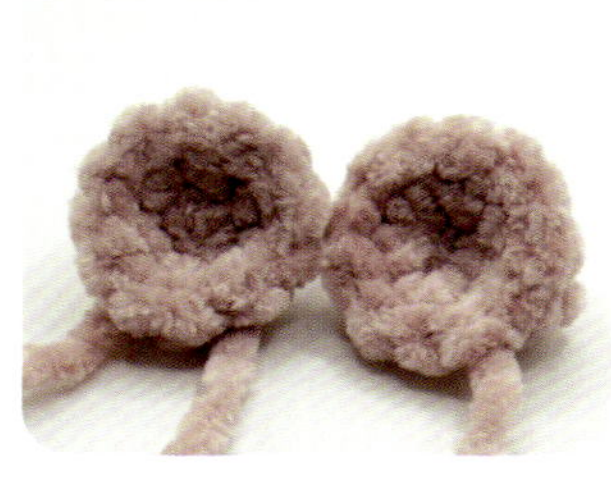

TAIL

Using B, work all stitches in a row.
Row 1: Ch 21, turn, sl st in the 2nd ch from the hook, sl st 19 (20 sts).
Fasten off and leave a long yarn tail for attaching later.

DETAILS AND ASSEMBLY

Using 3 pins, mark a V-shaped nose on the centre tip of the face between rounds 16 and 17. With the embroidery needle, push yarn C through the bottom of the head and out by the lower nose pin. Add one whip stitch up to one of the top pins (see page 18). Bring the needle horizontally through the nose to the second top pin and out. Sew the last whip stitch down through the lower pin spot where you first entered to complete the V shape. Push the yarn back through the same stitch on the bottom of the head, knot the two ends and weave the ends into the head.

Pin the ears to the top of the head between rounds 11 and 12 with 3 stitches separating them. Make sure both the ears are evenly spaced on the head and lined up with the safety eyes. Whip stitch them on using the embroidery needle and the yarn end from fastening off the ears. Weave the ends into the head.

Pin the tail between rounds 2 and 3 at the top of the back of the body. Once centred, use the embroidery needle and the long yarn tail to whip stitch the tail on. Weave in the end.

Details of how to outline the safety eyes and add the cheeks are on page 19.

PASCAL THE PARROT

Parrots are captivating pets known for their vibrant colours, acrobatic abilities and lively personalities. With proper training, these birds can mimic human speech, perform tricks and even sing songs. Although parrots can be noisy and messy, having a parrot like our Pascal offers entertainment and companionship for up to 80 years!

Finished size

3½in (9cm)

Supplies and materials

- Universal Yarn Bella Chenille, Super Bulky Weight, 100% Polyester, 131yds (120m) per 100g ball
  Yarn A Apple Red 117
  Yarn B Daffodil 102
  Yarn C Clover 111
  Yarn D Bright Salmon 106
- Hook size: 3.5mm (UK9:USE/4)
- 2 safety eyes ½in (14mm)
- Polyester fibre filling
- Embroidery needle
- Scissors
- Stitch markers
- Sewing pins

PARROT

Using A, work all stitches in a round from bottom to top. Stuff as you crochet.

Round 1: Make a MC with 12 dc (12 sts).
Round 2: (Dc, dc2inc) 6 times (18 sts).
Round 3: (Dc, dc2inc, dc) 6 times (24 sts).
Round 4: (Dc 3, dc2inc) 6 times (30 sts).
Round 5: Dc 25, (dc2inc) 5 times (35 sts).
Round 6: Dc in each st around (35 sts).
Round 7: Dc 25, (dc2tog) 5 times (30 sts).
Round 8: Dc 25, dc2tog, dc, dc2tog (28 sts).
Round 9: Dc 22, (dc2tog) 3 times (25 sts).
Round 10: Dc in each st around (25 sts).
Round 11: Dc 23, dc2tog (24 sts).

In the next round change to D for only the bobble stitch, then switch back to A for all of the dc stitches.

Round 12: Dc 12, BOB, dc 11 (24 sts).

Mark stitches 9 and 16 in round 12. These will be the 2 stitches where you place the safety eyes later in the pattern.

Rounds 13–15: Dc in each st around (24 sts).

Place safety eyes on round 12 in the marked stitches. They should be 3 stitches away from the sides of the beak.

Round 16: (Dc, dc2tog, dc) 6 times (18 sts).
Round 17: (Dc, dc2tog) 6 times (12 sts).
Round 18: (Dc, dc2tog) 4 times (8 sts).

Fasten off and weave the yarn under each of the front loops only, pull tight and hide the end inside the head.

WINGS

Make 2 wings using A. Work all stitches in a round.

Round 1: Make a MC with 6 dc (6 sts).

Round 2: (Dc2inc) twice, (change to B) (htr2inc) 3 times, (change to A) dc2inc (12 sts).

Round 3: Dc 4, (change to C) dc2inc, htr2inc, (tr2inc) twice, htr2inc, dc2inc, (change to A) dc 2 (18 sts).

Fasten off and leave a long yarn tail for attaching later. Cut and tie a knot in yarns C and B. These yarn ends will be hidden when the wings are sewn to the body.

DETAILS AND ASSEMBLY

Pin the wings to the side of the body between rounds 6 and 9 and past the safety eyes. The Clover colour of the wings needs to be near the tail and the Apple Red colour near the front of the body. Make sure both the wings are evenly spaced on the body. Whip stitch them on using the embroidery needle and the leftover yarn end from the fastening of the wing (see page 18). Start at the top, working around the rounded front half of the wing, but leave the back half of the wing not sewn. Weave the ends into the body.

Details of how to outline the safety eyes and add the cheeks are on page 19.

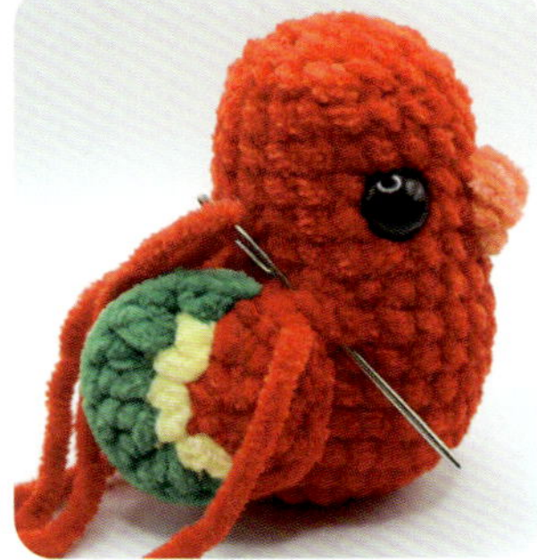

PICKLES THE POTBELLY PIG

Potbelly pigs are smart animals, similar to dogs, and can learn to do many tasks. Some can even swim! They are social creatures that need space and companionship, whether from humans or other pigs. Pickles' playful personality and love for rolling in the mud show the fun of having a potbelly pig as part of your family. Think about the joyful moments and affection that come with having such a charming companion.

Finished size

5in (12.5cm)

Supplies and materials

- Universal Yarn Bella Chenille, Super Bulky Weight, 100% Polyester, 131yds (120m) per 100g ball
  Yarn A Blush 127
  Yarn B Sugar Plum 108
- Hook size: 3.5mm (UK9:USE/4)
- 2 safety eyes ½in (14mm)
- Polyester fibre filling
- Embroidery needle
- Scissors
- Stitch markers
- Sewing pins

POTBELLY PIG

Using A, work all stitches in a round from front to back. Stuff as you crochet.

Round 1: Make a MC with 8 dc (8 sts).
Round 2: BLO dc in each st around (8 sts).
Change to B on the last stitch of round 2.
Round 3: (Dc2inc) 8 times (16 sts).
Round 4: (Dc, dc2inc) 8 times (24 sts).
Mark stitches 12 and 21 in round 4. These will be the 2 stitches where you place the safety eyes later in the pattern.
Round 5: Dc in each st around (24 sts).
Round 6: (Dc 3, dc2inc) 6 times (30 sts).
Add the safety eyes in the marked stitches on round 4. There should be 7 stitches between them.
Rounds 7–8: Dc in each st around (30 sts).
Change to A for each of the bobble stitches in the next round, then switch back to B for all of the dc stitches.
Round 9: Dc 2, BOB, dc 3, BOB, dc 5, (dc2tog, dc 2) 3 times, dc2tog, dc 4 (26 sts).
Round 10: Dc 14, dc2tog, dc 5, dc2tog, dc 3 (24 sts).
Round 11: Dc 13, dc2inc, dc, (dc2inc) 4 times, dc, dc2inc, dc 3 (30 sts).
Rounds 12–13: Dc in each st around (30 sts).
Change to A for each of the bobble stitches in the next round, then switch back to B for all of the dc stitches. The bobble stitches in round 14 should line up with the bobble stitches in round 9. If they don't, adjust them left or right by 1–2 stitches to get the correct placement.
Round 14: Dc 3, BOB, dc 3, BOB, dc 22 (30 sts).
Rounds 15–16: Dc in each st around (30 sts).
Round 17: (Dc 3, dc2tog) 6 times (24 sts).
Round 18: (Dc, dc2tog, dc) 6 times (18 sts).
Round 19: (Dc, dc2tog) 6 times (12 sts).
Round 20: (Dc, dc2tog) 4 times (8 sts).
Fasten off and weave the yarn under each of the front loops only, pull tight and hide the end inside the head.

TAIL

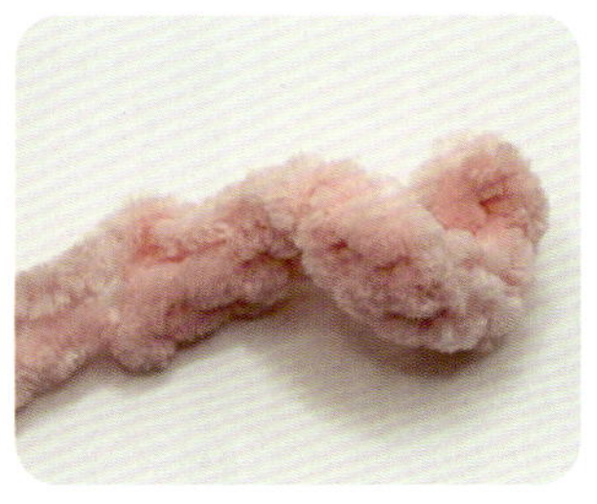

Using B, work all stitches in a row.
Row 1: Ch 11, turn, sl st in the 2nd ch from the hook, sl st 9 (10 sts).
Fasten off and leave a long yarn tail for attaching later.

EARS

Make 2 ears.

Using B, work all stitches in a row.

When turning, put the stitch in the 2nd ch from the hook.

Row 1: Start with a long yarn tail approximately 6in (15cm), ch 5, turn (5 sts).

Row 2: Dc in each st across, ch, turn (4 sts).

Row 3: (Dc2tog) twice, ch, turn (2 sts).

Row 4: Dc2tog, ch, turn (1 st).

Turn and work approximately 3 dc around the 3 sides of the ear, placing dc2inc in each of the 3 corners (15 sts). Fasten off and weave in the yarn end. The starting-yarn tail is for attaching the ears later.

DETAILS AND ASSEMBLY

Pin the ears to the top of the head between rounds 8 and 9, with 4 stitches separating them. Make sure both the ears are evenly spaced on the head and lined up with the safety eyes. Whip stitch them on using the embroidery needle and the yarn end from starting the ears (see page 18). Weave the ends into the head.

Pin the tail between rounds 18 and 19 at the top of the back of the body in the centre. Whip stitch the tail on with the embroidery needle and the long yarn tail, then weave in the end.

Details of how to outline the safety eyes and add the cheeks are on page 19.

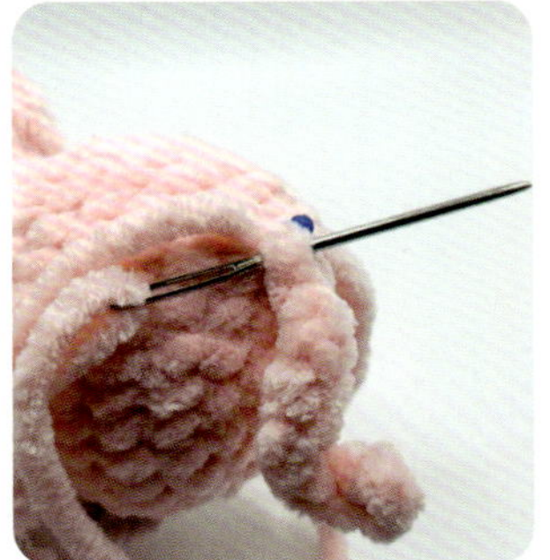

DUDLEY THE DACHSHUND

Dachshunds, also known as wiener or sausage dogs, are an energetic and affectionate miniature breed with a distinct long body and short legs. Dachshunds are known for forming strong bonds, and Dudley will melt your heart with his cuddles and endless need for attention.

Finished size

6½in (16.5cm)

Supplies and materials

- Premier Yarns Parfait Chunky, Super Bulky Weight, 100% Polyester, 131yds (120m) per 100g ball
  Yarn A Chocolate 35
  Yarn B Acorn 79
  Yarn C Black 10
- Hook size: 3.5mm (UK9:USE/4)
- 2 safety eyes ½in (14mm)
- Polyester fibre filling
- Embroidery needle
- Scissors
- Stitch markers
- Sewing pins
- Poly pellets (optional)

Please note: when doing multiple colour changes in a round, you can either cut and tie off the colours after every change or leave a loose running stitch.

DACHSHUND

Using A, work all stitches in a round from back to front. Stuff as you crochet and add poly pellets when instructed (see page 9).

Round 1: Make a MC with 12 dc (12 sts).
Round 2: (Dc, dc2inc) 6 times (18 sts).
Round 3: (Dc, dc2inc, dc) 6 times (24 sts).
Round 4: Dc in each st around (24 sts).
Change to B for each of the BOB stitches in the next 2 rounds, then switch back to A for the dc stitches.
Round 5: Dc 21, BOB, dc 2 (24 sts).
Round 6: Dc 3, BOB, dc 20 (24 sts).
Rounds 7–11: Dc in each st around (24 sts).
Change to B for each of the BOB stitches in the next 2 rounds, then switch back to A for the dc stitches.
Round 12: Dc 22, BOB, dc (24 sts).
Round 13: Dc 4, BOB, dc 19 (24 sts).
Optional: Add a small stocking with poly pellets to weight down the back end of the dog. Continue to stuff as you crochet.
Round 14: (Dc2tog) twice, dc 2, (dc2tog) twice, dc 3, dc2inc, dc, dc2inc, dc 3, (dc2tog) twice, dc (20 sts).
Round 15: Dc2tog, dc, dc2tog, dc 2, (dc2inc, dc 2) twice, dc2inc, dc 3, dc2tog, dc (20 sts).
Round 16: Dc 5, (dc2inc, dc) 5 times, dc2inc, dc 4 (26 sts).
Round 17: (Dc2tog) twice, dc 6, (dc2inc, dc 2) 3 times, dc2inc, dc 4, dc2tog (27 sts).
Round 18: Dc in each st around (27 sts).
Round 19: (Dc2inc) 3 times, dc 22, (dc2inc) twice (32 sts).
The decreases in round 20 should be centred on the top of the head, lining up with the increases from round 17. If they don't, adjust them right or left by 1–2 stitches.
Round 20: Dc 10, (dc2tog, dc 2) 3 times, dc2tog, dc 8 (28 sts).
Round 21: Dc 5, dc2tog, dc 3, change to B dc 2, dc2tog, change to A dc 3, change to B dc, dc2tog, dc, change to A dc 4, dc2tog, dc (24 sts).
Mark stitches 11 and 18 in round 22. These will be the 2 stitches where you will place the safety eyes later in the pattern.
Round 22: Dc in each st around (24 sts).
Round 23: Dc 8, (dc2tog, dc) 3 times, dc2tog, dc 5 (20 sts).
Round 24: Dc in each st around (20 sts).
Add the safety eyes in the marked stitches on round 22. There should be 6 stitches between them, with the 3 B stitches centred above each of the safety eyes. If not, adjust them 1–2 stitches left or right to get the correct placement.
Round 25: Dc 2, (dc2tog, dc) twice, dc2tog, dc 5, dc2tog, dc, dc2tog (15 sts).
Round 26: (Dc2tog) twice dc 9, dc2tog (12 sts).
Round 27: (Dc, dc2tog) 4 times (8 sts).
Fasten off and weave the yarn under each of the FLO, pull tight and hide the end inside the head.

TAIL

Using A, work all stitches in a row.
Row 1: Ch 8, turn, sl st in the 2nd ch from the hook, sl st 3, dc 3 (7 sts).
Fasten off and leave a long yarn tail for attaching later.

EARS

Make 2 ears using A. Work all stitches in a round.
Do not stuff.
Round 1: Make a MC with 6 dc (6 sts).
Round 2: (Dc2inc) 6 times (12 sts).
Round 3: (Dc, dc2inc) 6 times (18 sts).
Round 4: (Dc, dc2inc, dc) 6 times (24 sts).
Rounds 5–6: Dc in each st around (24 sts).
Round 7: (Dc, dc2tog, dc) 6 times (18 sts).
Rounds 8–9: Dc in each st around (18 sts).
Round 10: (Dc, dc2tog) 6 times (12 sts).
Rounds 11–12: Dc in each st around (12 sts).
Round 13: (Dc, dc2tog) 4 times (8 sts).

Pinch the opening closed, dc through both sides with 4 dc and close the opening (4 sts).
Fasten off and leave a long yarn tail for attaching later.

DETAILS AND ASSEMBLY

Using pins, mark the width of the nose in the centre of the face between rounds 25 and 26 and 3 stitches apart. With the embroidery needle and C, push the yarn through the side of the head to the first nose pin. Whip stitch at least 3 stitches between the two pins to make the nose. Push the yarn back through the same stitch on the side of the head and knot the two ends. Weave the ends into the head.

Pin the ears to the side of the head between rounds 16 and 20 with 1 stitch before the middle B stitch above the safety eye. Make sure both the ears are evenly spaced. Whip stitch them on using the embroidery needle and the yarn end from closing the ears. Sew along the seam, then bring the needle up through the head to the side of the neck at round 16. Add a whip stitch to the back edge of the ear to secure it to the side of the head to prevent it from flopping around. Weave the ends into the head.

Pin the tail between rounds 2 and 3 at the top of the back of the body. Once centred with the back BOB stitches, use the embroidery needle and the long yarn tail to whip stitch the tail on. Weave the ends into the body.

Details of how to outline the safety eyes and add the cheeks are on page 19.

TURBO THE TORTOISE

One of the longest-living pets is the tortoise. They usually live between 50 and 100 years and are relatively easy to care for, although they do require a significant amount of dedication. Turbo the Tortoise enjoys spending most of the year munching on a healthy diet of garden weeds and vegetables before hibernating during the colder months.

Finished size

5½in (14cm)

Supplies and materials

- Premier Yarns Parfait Chunky, Super Bulky Weight, 100% Polyester, 131yds (120m) per 100g ball
  Yarn A Teddy Bear 36
- Universal Yarn Bella Chenille, Super Bulky Weight, 100% Polyester, 131yds (120m) per 100g ball
  Yarn B Clover 111
- Hook size: 3.5mm (UK9:USE/4)
- 2 safety eyes ½in (14mm)
- Polyester fibre filling
- Embroidery needle
- Scissors
- Stitch markers
- Sewing pins

HEAD

Using B, work all stitches in a round from top to bottom. Stuff as you crochet.
Round 1: Make a MC with 8 dc (8 sts).
Round 2: (Dc, dc2inc) 4 times (12 sts).
Round 3: Dc 3, (dc2inc) 6 times, dc 3 (18 sts).
Round 4: Dc in each st around (18 sts).
Round 5: (Dc, dc2inc, dc) 6 times (24 sts).
Mark stitches 9 and 18 in round 5. These will be the 2 stitches where you place the safety eyes later in the pattern.
Round 6: Dc in each st around (24 sts).
Round 7: Dc 3, (dc2tog, dc) 5 times, dc2tog, dc 4 (18 sts).
Place safety eyes on round 5 in the marked stitches, with 8 stitches between them, making sure that the increases are centred between each of the safety eyes.
Round 8: (Dc, dc2tog) 6 times (12 sts).
Rounds 9–10: Dc in each st around (12 sts).
Pinch the opening closed. If the seam is not centred and horizontal with the safety eyes, increase or decrease 1–2 stitches.
Dc through both sides with 6 dc and close the opening (6 sts).
Fasten off and leave a long yarn tail for attaching later.

SHELL

Using A, work all stitches in a round from bottom to top. Stuff as you crochet.
Round 1: Make a MC with 12 dc (12 sts).
Round 2: (Dc, dc2inc) 6 times (18 sts).
Round 3: (Dc, dc2inc, dc) 6 times (24 sts).
Change to B for each of the bobble stitches in the next round, then switch back to A for all of the dc stitches.
Round 4: Dc, BOB, dc, dc2inc, dc 2, BOB, dc2inc, dc 3, dc2inc, dc, BOB, dc, dc2inc, dc 2, BOB, dc2inc, dc 3, dc2inc (30 sts).
Round 5: (Dc 2, dc2inc, dc2) 6 times (36 sts).
Round 6: Dc in each st around (36 sts).
Fasten off and weave in the yarn ends.
Attach A to the back loop only of the 1st stitch of round 6.
Round 7: BLO dc in each st around (36 sts).
Round 8: (Dc 2, dc2tog, dc2) 6 times (30 sts).
Round 9: Dc in each st around (30 sts).
Round 10: (Dc 3, dc2tog) 6 times (24 sts).
Round 11: (Dc, dc2tog, dc) 6 times (18 sts).
Round 12: (Dc, dc2tog) 6 times (12 sts).
Round 13: (Dc, dc2tog) 4 times (8 sts).
Fasten off and weave the yarn under each of the front loops only, pull tight and hide the end inside the shell.

TAIL

Using B, work all stitches in a row.

Row 1: Ch 5, turn, dc in the 2nd ch from the hook, dc 3 (4 sts).

Fasten off and leave a long yarn tail for attaching later.

DETAILS AND ASSEMBLY

Flip the tortoise over and attach A to the 1st FLO on round 6. Then, dc across the remaining 35 front loop only stitches on the same round. This creates an edging on the tortoise shell. Fasten off and weave the yarn ends into the shell.

Pin the head between rounds 5 and 6 in the space between the first 2 bobble stitches. This is the smaller space that has 5 stitches separating the bobble stitches. Make sure the head is evenly centred and lines up with the bobble stitches on the rounds below it. Whip stitch it on using the embroidery needle (see page 18) and the leftover yarn end from closing the head.

Bring the embroidery needle up through the top of the neck between rounds 9 and 10 to add an extra whip stitch to the yarn A edging on the shell. This secures the head in place against the shell.

Pin the tail to between rounds 6 and 7, centred between the back 2 bobble stitches. Whip stitch the tail on with the embroidery needle and the long yarn tail. Weave in the end.

Details of how to outline the safety eyes and add the cheeks are on page 19.

BENNY THE BUDGIE

Budgies, one of the most popular pet birds, are among the smallest members of the parrot family. These social birds mate for life and require ample mental and physical stimulation due to their high intelligence! So, after crocheting your own Benny the Budgie, be sure to provide some games and foraging toys to keep your new friend engaged and happy.

Finished size

3½in (9cm)

Supplies and materials

- Universal Yarn Bella Chenille, Super Bulky Weight, 100% Polyester, 131yds (120m) per 100g ball
  Yarn A Snowy 101
  Yarn B Ocean 105
  Yarn C Daffodil 102
- Hook size: 3.5mm (UK9:USE/4)
- 2 safety eyes ½in (14mm)
- Polyester fibre filling
- Embroidery needle
- Scissors
- Stitch markers
- Sewing pins

BUDGIE

Using B, work all stitches in a round from bottom to top. Stuff as you crochet.

Round 1: Make a MC with 12 dc (12 sts).
Round 2: (Dc, dc2inc) 6 times (18 sts).
Round 3: (Dc, dc2inc, dc) 6 times (24 sts).
Round 4: (Dc 3, dc2inc) 6 times (30 sts).
Round 5: Dc 25, (dc2inc) 5 times (35 sts).
Round 6: Dc in each st around (35 sts).
Round 7: Dc 25, (dc2tog) 5 times (30 sts).
Round 8: Dc 25, dc2tog, dc, dc2tog (28 sts).
Round 9: Dc 22, (dc2tog) 3 times (25 sts).
Fasten off and weave in the yarn ends.
Attach A to the last stitch of round 9.
Round 10: Dc in each st around (25 sts).
Round 11: Dc 23, dc2tog (24 sts).

In the next round change to C for only the bobble stitch, then switch back to A for all of the dc stitches.
Round 12: Dc 12, BOB, dc 11 (24 sts).
Mark stitches 9 and 16 in round 12. These will be the 2 stitches where you place the safety eyes later in the pattern.
Rounds 13–15: Dc in each st around (24 sts).
Place safety eyes on round 12 in the marked stitches. They should be 3 stitches away from the sides of the beak.
Round 16: (Dc, dc2tog, dc) 6 times (18 sts).
Round 17: (Dc, dc2tog) 6 times (12 sts).
Round 18: (Dc, dc2tog) 4 times (8 sts).
Fasten off and weave the yarn under each of the front loops only, pull tight and hide the end inside the head.

WINGS

Make 2 wings using B. Work all stitches in a round.
Round 1: Make a MC with 6 dc (6 sts).
Round 2: (Dc2inc) twice, (htr, tr) in the next st, ch 1, (tr, htr) in the next st, (dc2inc) twice (12 sts).
Fasten off and leave a long yarn tail for attaching later.

DETAILS AND ASSEMBLY

Pin the wings to the side of the body between rounds 6 and 9 and past the cheek detail. The point of the wings needs to be near the tail and the rounded end near the front of the body. Make sure both the wings are evenly spaced on the body. When pinned correctly, whip stitch them on using the embroidery needle and the leftover yarn end from fastening off the wing (see page 18). Start at the top, working around the rounded front half of the wing, but leave the back half of the wing not sewn. Weave the ends into the body.

Details of how to outline the safety eyes and add the cheeks are on page 19.

TANGLE THE TABBY

Tabby cats are the most well-known domestic cats and make wonderful companions for individuals and families. They are intelligent, can learn tricks and respond to training cues, and have a distinctive fur pattern and markings on their foreheads, contributing to their wild-looking appearance. Our adorable little furball, Tangle, is no exception. He will steal your heart with his charm, making him truly special and one of a kind!

Finished size

5in (12.5cm)

Supplies and materials

- Premier Yarns Parfait Chunky, Super Bulky Weight, 100% Polyester, 131yds (120m) per 100g ball
  Yarn A Maize 74
  Yarn B Mango 11
  Yarn C Cream 07
  Yarn D Cotton Candy 03
- Hook size: 3.5mm (UK9:USE/4)
- 2 safety eyes ½in (14mm)
- Polyester fibre filling
- Embroidery needle
- Scissors
- Stitch markers
- Sewing pins

Please note: when doing multiple colour changes in a round, you can either cut and tie off the colours after every change or leave a loose running stitch.

TABBY CAT

Using A, work all stitches in a round from bottom to top. Stuff as you crochet.

Round 1: Make a MC with 12 dc (12 sts).
Round 2: (Dc, dc2inc) 6 times (18 sts).
Round 3: (Dc, dc2inc, dc) 6 times (24 sts).
Round 4: Dc 3, dc2inc, dc, BOB, dc, dc2inc, dc, change to C BOB, change to A dc, (dc2inc) twice, dc, change to C BOB, change to A dc, dc2inc, dc, BOB, dc, dc2inc, dc 3 (30 sts).
Round 5: Dc in each st around (30 sts).
Round 6: Dc 5, change to B dc 8, change to A dc 4, change to B dc 8, change to A dc 5 (30 sts).
Round 7: Dc in each st around (30 sts).
Round 8: Dc 5, change to B dc 8, change to A dc 4, change to B dc 8, change to A dc 5 (30 sts).
Round 9: (Dc 3, dc2tog) 6 times (24 sts).
Round 10: FLO (dc 3, dc2inc) 6 times (30 sts).
Round 11: Dc 11, FLO dc 9, dc 10 (30 sts).
Round 12: Dc 14, change to C BOB, dc, BOB, change to A dc 13 (30 sts).

Mark stitches 14 and 19 in round 13. These will be the 2 stitches where you will place the safety eyes later in the pattern.

Round 13: Dc 6, change to B dc 6, change to A dc 2, change to C dc 3, change to A dc 2, change to B dc 6, change to A dc 5 (30 sts).

The single Cream dc stitch in round 14 should be centred between the 2 BOB stitches from round 12. If it is not, please adjust it right or left by 1 stitch.

Round 14: Dc 15, change to C dc, change to A dc 14 (30 sts).

Round 15: Dc 7, change to B dc 4, change to A dc 9, change to B dc 4, change to A dc 6 (30 sts).

Add the safety eyes in the marked stitches on round 13. There should be 4 stitches between them.

Round 16: (Dc 3, dc2tog) 6 times (24 sts).
Round 17: (Dc, dc2tog, dc) 6 times (18 sts).
Round 18: (Dc, dc2tog) 6 times (12 sts).
Round 19: (Dc, dc2tog) 4 times (8 sts).

Fasten off and weave the yarn under each of the FLO, pull tight and hide the end inside the head.

EARS

Make 2 ears using A. Work all stitches in a row. When turning, put the stitch in the 2nd ch from the hook.

Row 1: Start with a long yarn tail approximately 6in (15cm), ch 5, turn (5 sts).
Row 2: Dc in each st across, ch turn (4 sts).
Row 3: (Dc2tog) twice, ch, turn (2 sts).
Row 4: Dc in each st across, ch turn (2 sts).
Row 5: Dc2tog, ch turn (1 st).

Turn and work a dc2inc in the last decrease then 4 dc along the first side of the ear, dc2inc in the corner, dc 2 along the bottom of the ear, dc2inc in the 3rd corner, 4 dc up the last side of the ear. Fasten off and weave the yarn end down through the bottom of the ear (approx. 16 sts). The starting yarn tail is for attaching the ears later.

TAIL

Using B, work all stitches in a round.
Stuff as you crochet.
Round 1: Make a MC with 6 dc (6 sts).
Round 2: (Dc, dc2inc, dc) twice (8 sts).
Change to A on the last stitch of round 2.
Round 3: (Dc, dc2inc) 4 times (12 sts).
Round 4: Dc in each st around (12 sts).
Change to B on the last stitch of round 4.
Rounds 5-6: Dc in each st around (12 sts).
Change to A on the last stitch of round 6.
Round 7: (Dc2inc) 3 times, dc 9 (15 sts).
Round 8: Dc 7, (dc2tog) 3 times, dc 2 (12 sts).
Change to B on the last stitch of round 8.
Round 9: Dc 2, (dc2inc) 3 times, dc 7 (15 sts).
Round 10: Dc 9, (dc2tog) 3 times (12 sts).
Change to A on the last stitch of round 10.
Round 11: Dc 4, (dc2inc) 3 times, dc 5 (15 sts).
In the next round, the last decrease will overlap onto the starting stitch of that round. This will move your new starting stitch over by 1 stitch.

Round 12: Dc 9, (dc2tog) 3 times (12 sts).
Round 13: Dc in each st around (12 sts).
Round 14: Dc 9, htr 3 (12 sts).
Round 15: (Dc, dc2tog) 4 times (8 sts).
Pinch the opening closed, dc through both sides with 4 dc and close the opening (4 sts).
Fasten off and leave a long yarn tail for attaching later.

DETAILS AND ASSEMBLY

With the embroidery needle and D, push the yarn through the side of the head and out at the Cream stitch between the BOB stitches on the face. Make about 6 whip stitches around that stitch until the nose is a little puffy. Bring the needle back through the same stitch on the side of the head, knot the two ends and weave the ends into the head.

Pin the ears to the top of the head with the seam between rounds 15 and 19, 1–2 stitches apart. The bottom seam of the ears should be 5 stitches past the safety eyes. Make sure both the ears are evenly spaced on the head. Whip stitch them on at the front of the ear, sewing along the bottom seam with the embroidery needle and the starting yarn end. Weave the ends into the head.

Pin the seam of the tail between rounds 4 and 7 on the lower back, centred but at an angle so the tail is not directly behind the cat's body. Once centred correctly, use the embroidery needle and long yarn tail to whip stitch the tail on. Weave the needle through the back 2–3 rounds up and add an extra whip stitch or two to keep the tail in place. Weave in the end.

Details of how to outline the safety eyes and add the cheeks are on page 19.

BUBBLES THE BETTA FISH

The betta fish is a vibrant and charming aquatic pet known for forming bonds with its guardians and even learning tricks. As territorial creatures, betta fish should be kept alone in a tank to prevent conflicts with others. Our little betta, Bubbles, with his full, flowing fins and lively personality, is truly a delight to watch.

Finished size

4in (10cm)

Supplies and materials

- Universal Yarn Bella Chenille, Super Bulky Weight, 100% Polyester 131yds (120m) per 100g ball
  Yarn A Sweet Lilac 103
  Yarn B Pansy Purple 116
- Hook size: 3.5mm (UK9:USE/4)
- 2 safety eyes ½in (14mm)
- Polyester fibre filling
- Embroidery needle
- Scissors
- Stitch markers
- Sewing pins

BETTA FISH

Using A, work all stitches in a round from front to back. Stuff as you crochet.

Round 1: Make a MC with 6 dc (6 sts).

Round 2: (Dc, dc2inc) 3 times (9 sts).

Round 3: (Dc2inc) 9 times (18 sts).

Round 4: Dc in each st around (18 sts).

Round 5: (Dc, dc2inc, dc) 6 times (24 sts).

Mark stitches 3 and 13 in round 5. These will be the 2 stitches where you will place the safety eyes later in the pattern.

Rounds 6–8: Dc in each st around (24 sts).

Add the safety eyes in the marked stitches on round 5. There should be 9 stitches between them.

Round 9: (Dc, dc2tog, dc) 6 times (18 sts).

Round 10: Dc in each st around (18 sts).

Round 11: (Dc, dc2tog) 6 times (12 sts).

Round 12: Dc in each st around (12 sts).

Change colour to B on the last stitch of round 12.

Pinch the opening closed. If the seam is not centred with the middle of the safety eyes, increase or decrease 1–2 stitches.

Dc2inc (6 times) through both sides and close the opening, ch 3, turn (12 sts).

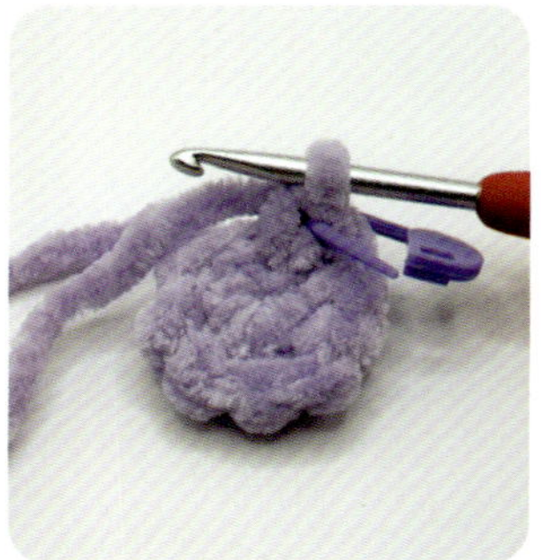

TAIL

Row 1: (Dtr2inc) 12 times, ch 2, sl st to the same stitch as the last dtr (24 sts).

Fasten off and weave in the ends.

BOTTOM FIN

Using B, work all stitches in a row.
After turning, work back the other way, placing the first st in the 3rd st from the hook.

Row 1: Ch 5, turn (5 sts).

Row 2: Tr2inc, dtr2inc, tr, ch 2, sl st to the same stitch as the last tr (5 sts).

Fasten off and leave a long yarn tail for attaching later.

TOP FIN

Using B, work all stitches in a row.
After each row, turn and work back the other way, placing the first st in the 4th st from the hook.

Row 1: Ch 7, turn (7 sts).

Row 2: (Dtr2inc) twice, tr2inc, tr, ch 2, sl st to the same stitch as the last tr (7 sts).

Fasten off and leave a long yarn tail for attaching later.

DETAILS AND ASSEMBLY

Pin the bottom fin to the underside of the body starting between rounds 5 and 6 and ending 2 rounds before the tail at rounds 10 and 11. Make sure the bottom fin is evenly spaced between the safety eyes and lining up with the tail. Whip stitch it on using the embroidery needle (see page 18) and the leftover yarn end from the fin. Weave the ends into the body.

Before sewing, pin the top fin to the fish beginning at rounds 5 and 6, directly above the bottom fin with the double treble stitches placed by the back fin. End between rounds 10 and 11, 2 rounds before the tail. When pinned centred, whip stitch the top fin on to the top of the fish body, using the embroidery needle and the leftover yarn end. Weave the ends into the body.

Details of how to outline the safety eyes and add the cheeks are on page 19.

CAPTAIN THE CAPYBARA

The capybara is the largest rodent in the world and is often called a 'giant guinea pig'. These gentle animals are shy, not aggressive, don't shed and love being around other capybaras. Because of their size, they need a lot of food and a big space with dry land and water to swim in. That's not the case with Captain. Our capybara would be happy in any room of your home, doesn't need water and will thrive on your love and attention!

Finished size

4½in (11.5cm)

Supplies and materials

- Premier Yarns Parfait Chunky, Super Bulky Weight, 100% Polyester, 131yds (120m) per 100g ball
  Yarn A Acorn 79
  Yarn B Chocolate 35
- Hook size: 3.5mm (UK9:USE/4)
- 2 safety eyes ½in (14mm)
- Polyester fibre filling
- Embroidery needle
- Scissors
- Stitch markers
- Sewing pins

Please note: when doing multiple colour changes in a round, you can either cut and tie off the colours after every change or leave a loose running stitch.

CAPYBARA

Using A, work all stitches in a round from bottom to top. Stuff as you crochet.

Round 1: Make a MC with 12 dc (12 sts).

Round 2: Dc 3, (dc2inc) 3 times, dc 3, (dc2inc) 3 times (18 sts).

Round 3: Dc 4, (dc2inc, dc) twice, dc2inc, dc 4, (dc2inc, dc) twice, dc2inc (24 sts).

Change to B for each of the BOB stitches in the next round, then switch back to A for the dc stitches.

Round 4: Dc 4, dc2inc, (dc, BOB) in the same st, dc2inc, dc 2, dc2inc, (BOB, dc) in the same st, dc2inc, dc 4, dc2inc, (dc, BOB) in the same st, dc2inc, dc 2, dc2inc, (BOB, dc) in the same st, dc2inc (36 sts).

Rounds 5–8: Dc in each st around (36 sts).

Round 9: Dc 24, (dc2tog) twice, dc 4, (dc2tog) twice (32 sts).

Round 10: Dc 10, FLO (dc2inc, dc) twice, FLO dc2inc, dc 9, dc2tog, dc 4, dc2tog (33 sts).

Round 11: Dc 7, dc2tog, dc 2, FLO (dc2inc) 5 times, dc 2, dc2tog, dc 6, (dc2tog) twice, dc, dc2tog (33 sts).

Round 12: Dc2tog, dc 10, change to B dc 7, change to A dc 10, (dc2tog) twice (30 sts).

Round 13: (Dc2tog) twice, dc 7, change to B dc 7, change to A dc 8, (dc2tog) twice (26 sts).

Round 14: Dc2tog, dc 7, change to B dc 7, change to A dc 8, dc2tog (24 sts).

Mark stitches 7 and 18 in round 15. These will be the 2 stitches where you will place the safety eyes later in the pattern.

Round 15: Dc 8, change to B dc 7, change to A dc 9 (24 sts).

Round 16: Dc 8, change to B dc2tog, dc 3, dc2tog, change to A dc 9 (22 sts).

Round 17: Dc in each st around (22 sts).

Add the safety eyes in the marked stitches on round 15. There should be 10 stitches between them, and they should be 1 stitch away from the Chocolate nose colour.

Round 18: Dc2tog, dc 4, dc2tog, dc 5, dc2tog, dc 5, dc2tog (18 sts).

Round 19: Dc in each st around (18 sts).

Round 20: (Dc, dc2tog) 6 times (12 sts).

Round 21: (Dc, dc2tog) 4 times (8 sts).

Fasten off and weave the yarn under each of the FLO, pull tight and hide the end inside the head.

EARS

Make 2 ears using B. Work all stitches in a round.
Round 1: Make a MC with 5 dc (5 sts).
Fasten off and leave a long yarn tail for attaching later.

DETAILS AND ASSEMBLY

Pin the ears to the side of the head between rounds 17 and 19 and 2 stitches past the safety eyes. Make sure the ears are evenly spaced on the head and facing forwards. Whip stitch the bottom of them on using the embroidery needle and the leftover yarn end. Weave the ends into the head.

Details of how to outline the safety eyes and add the cheeks are on page 19.

REUBEN THE RABBIT

Rabbits are enjoyable and friendly pets with distinct personalities. They are affectionate and gentle, forming strong bonds with their owners. Rabbits express their love and excitement through binkies, zoomies and snuggles. A rabbit can be a wonderful pet choice, especially our little Reuben, who is exceptionally quiet and very clean.

Finished size

6in (15cm)

Supplies and materials

- Universal Yarn Bella Chenille, Super Bulky Weight, 100% Polyester, 131yds (120m) per 100g ball
  Yarn A Sesame 120
  Yarn B Blush 127
  Yarn C Chocolate 123
- Hook size: 3.5mm (UK9:USE/4)
- 2 safety eyes ½in (14mm)
- Polyester fibre filling
- Embroidery needle
- Scissors
- Stitch markers
- Sewing pins

RABBIT

Using A, work all stitches in a round from bottom to top. Stuff as you crochet.

Round 1: Make a MC with 12 dc (12 sts).
Round 2: (Dc, dc2inc) 6 times (18 sts).
Round 3: (Dc, dc2inc, dc) 6 times (24 sts).
Change to B for each of the bobble stitches in the next round, then switch to A on the dc stitches.
Round 4: (Dc 3, dc2inc) twice, dc, BOB, dc, (dc2inc) twice, dc, BOB, dc, (dc2inc, dc 3) twice (30 sts).
Rounds 5–7: Dc in each st around (30 sts).
Change to B for each of the bobble stitches in the next round, then switch to A on the dc stitches.
The bobble stitches in round 8 should line up with the bobble stitches in round 4. If they don't, adjust them left or right by 1–2 stitches to get the correct placement.
Round 8: Dc 11, BOB, dc 6, BOB, dc 11 (30 sts).
Round 9: Dc 9, (dc2tog) 6 times, dc 9 (24 sts).
Round 10: Dc 9 FLO (dc2inc) 6 times, dc 9 (30 sts).
Rounds 11–12: Dc in each st around (30 sts).
Round 13: Dc 9, (dc2tog) 6 times, dc 9 (24 sts).
Mark stitches 10 and 16 in round 13. These will be the 2 stitches where you will place the safety eyes later in the pattern.
Rounds 14–15: Dc in each st around (24 sts).
Add the safety eyes in the marked stitches on round 13. There should be 4 stitches between them.
Round 16: Dc in each st around (24 sts).
Round 17: (Dc, dc2tog, dc) 6 times (18 sts).
Round 18: (Dc, dc2tog) 6 times (12 sts).
Round 19: (Dc, dc2tog) 4 times (8 sts).
Fasten off and weave the yarn under each of the front loops only, pull tight and hide the end inside the head.

TAIL

Using A, work all stitches in a round.
Do not stuff. This step will come during the assembly.

Round 1: Make a MC with 6 dc (6 sts).
Round 2: (Dc2inc) 6 times (12 sts).
Round 3: (Dc, dc2inc) 6 times (18 sts).
Round 4: Dc in each st around (18 sts).
Fasten off and leave a long tail for attaching later.

EARS

Make 2 ears using A. Work all stitches in a round.
Do not stuff.

Round 1: Make a MC with 6 dc (6 sts).
Round 2: (Dc2inc) 6 times (12 sts).
Round 3: (Dc, dc2inc) 6 times (18 sts).
Rounds 4–5: Dc in each st around (18 sts).
Round 6: (Dc, dc2tog) 6 times (12 sts).
Round 7: Dc in each st around (12 sts).
Round 8: (Dc, dc2tog) 4 times (8 sts).

Pinch the opening closed, dc through both sides with 4 dc and close the opening (4 sts).
Fasten off and leave a long tail for attaching later.

DETAILS AND ASSEMBLY

Using 3 pins, mark a V-shaped nose in the centre of the face between rounds 12 and 13, 4 stitches apart. With the embroidery needle and C push the yarn through the bottom of the head and out at the lower nose pin. Add one whip stitch up to one of the top pins, bring the needle horizontally through the nose to the second top pin and out. Add the last whip stitch down through the lower pin spot where you first entered to complete the V shape. Push the yarn back through the same stitch on the bottom of the head, knot the two ends, and weave the ends into the head.

Pin the ears to the side of the head with the seam between rounds 14 and 15, 2 stitches past the safety eyes. Make sure both the ears are evenly spaced on the head. Whip stitch them on using the embroidery needle and the leftover yarn end. Sew along the seam, then bring the needle up through the top of the head and add a whip stitch to the back of the ear. This is to secure it to the top of the head and prevent it from flopping over. Weave the ends into the head.

Pin the tail to the lower back of the body, starting between rounds 3 and 4 and ending between rounds 8 and 9. Make sure it is centred on the lower back and that the rabbit can sit properly. Whip stitch it on using the embroidery needle and the leftover yarn end. Start at the bottom of the tail and work around in a circle. Before closing the last 4 whip stitches, stuff the tail to ensure it keeps its shape. Weave the ends into the head.

Details of how to outline the safety eyes and add the cheeks are on 19.

REMINGTON THE RHINOCEROS BEETLE

Bugs can make great pets, and one interesting example is the horned rhinoceros beetle. This beetle has a single large horn that it uses for defence against predators, as it does not bite. While these fascinating creatures do not enjoy being held, they are easy to care for. However, their lifespan is relatively short, typically living only two to three months after metamorphosis, but not Remington. He will gladly be a snuggly pet for years to come.

Finished size

6in (15cm)

Supplies and materials

- Premier Yarns Parfait Chunky, Super Bulky Weight, 100% Polyester, 131yds (120m) per 100g ball
  Yarn A Teddy Bear 36
  Yarn B Cornflower 40
- Hook size: 3.5mm (UK9:USE/4)
- 2 safety eyes ¾in (18mm)
- Polyester fibre filling
- Embroidery needle
- Scissors
- Stitch markers
- Sewing pins

BEETLE

Using A, work all stitches in a round from bottom to top. Stuff as you crochet.

Round 1: Make a MC with 12 dc (12 sts).
Round 2: (Dc, dc2inc) 6 times (18 sts).
Round 3: (Dc, dc2inc, dc) 6 times (24 sts).
Rounds 4–9: Dc in each st around (24 sts).
Round 10: (Dc, dc2tog, dc) 6 times (18 sts).
Round 11: FLO (dc, dc2inc, dc) 6 times (24 sts).
Mark stitches 7 and 19 in round 12. These will be the 2 stitches where you will place the safety eyes later in the pattern.
Rounds 12–13: Dc in each st around (24 sts).
Round 14: Dc 12, BOB, dc 9, dc2tog (23 sts).
Add the safety eyes in the marked stitches on round 12. There should be 11 stitches between them. If the safety eyes are not even or spaced correctly with the bobble stitch, adjust 1–2 stitches to the right or left.
Round 15: (Dc2tog) twice, dc 17, htr 2 (21 sts).
Round 16: Htr 3, dc 2, (dc2tog, dc 3) twice, dc2tog, dc 2, htr 2 (18 sts).
The next rounds with sl st and FLO sts will shift left or right to line up with the BOB sts on the top of the head.
Round 17: Htr 3, dc 3, FLO sl st 7 only, dc 3, dc2tog (17 sts).
Round 18: Dc, dc2tog, dc 5, dc2inc, dc, dc2inc, dc 6 (18 sts).
Round 19: Dc2tog, dc, dc2tog, dc 10, dc2tog, htr (15 sts).
Round 20: Htr 3, (dc2tog) twice, FLO sl st 4 only, (dc2tog) twice (11 sts).
Round 21: Htr 3, FLO dc 7, htr (11 sts).
Round 22: Htr 4, dc2tog, FLO dc 3, dc2tog (9 sts).
Round 23: (Dc2tog) twice, FLO dc 5 (7 sts).
Rounds 24–25: Dc in each st around (7 sts).
Fasten off and weave the yarn under each of the FLO, pull tight and hide the end inside the head.

LEGS

Make 6 legs using A. Work all stitches in a row. When turning, put the first stitch in the 2nd ch from the hook.

Row 1: Ch 5, turn (5 sts).
Row 2: Sl st in each st across (4 sts).
Fasten off and leave a long yarn tail for attaching later.

WINGS

Make 2 wings using B. Work all stitches in a round.
Do not stuff.

Round 1: Make a MC with 8 dc (8 sts).
Round 2: (Dc2inc) 8 times (16 sts).
Round 3: (Dc, dc2inc) 8 times (24 sts).
Rounds 4–5: Dc in each st around (24 sts).
Round 6: Dc 7, (dc2tog, dc) 3 times, dc2tog, dc 6 (20 sts).
Round 7: Dc 8, dc2tog, dc, dc2tog, dc 7 (18 sts).
Round 8: Dc in each st around (18 sts).
Pinch the opening closed, dc through both sides with 9 dc and close the opening (9 sts).
Fasten off and leave a long yarn tail for attaching later.

DETAILS AND ASSEMBLY

Pin the wings side by side between rounds 10 and 11 on the top of the back between the safety eyes. Make sure they are evenly centred behind the BOB stitch on the head with the decreases facing to the outside of the beetle. Use the leftover yarn end from closing the wings and the embroidery needle to whip stitch them in place along the seams. Bring the embroidery needle and yarn end up through one of the wings near round 9 where the wings meet. Sew the wings together by adding a whip stitch on every other round, zigzagging back and forth until round 5. Weave the ends into the wings.

Pin two of the six legs to the underside of the beetle's body between rounds 9 and 10 with 2 stitches between them and 2 stitches from each of the wings. Whip stitch them on using the embroidery needle and the yarn ends from each of the legs. Knot both yarn ends together from each leg and weave them into the body.

Pin the next two legs between rounds 7 and 8 with 2 stitches between them and below the first 2 legs. Whip stitch them on. Knot both yarn ends together from each leg and weave them into the body. Repeat these steps for the last two legs, whip stitching them on between rounds 5 and 6. Knot and weave in all the ends.

Details of how to outline the safety eyes and add the cheeks are on page 19.

COCONUT THE COCKATIEL

Cockatiels belong to the parrot family and are social birds that enjoy the company of others, whether it's with fellow cockatiels or their human companions. By using positive reinforcement, you can train them to perform tricks like singing and dancing. Coconut, a cheerful little cockatiel, loves to perch on shoulders, enjoys hand-fed snacks and learning show tunes.

Finished size

3½in (9cm)

Supplies and materials

- Universal Yarn Bella Chenille, Super Bulky Weight, 100% Polyester, 131yds (120m) per 100g ball
  Yarn A Misty 119
  Yarn B Snowy 101
  Yarn C Daffodil 102
  Yarn D Sesame 120
- Hook size: 3.5mm (UK9:USE/4)
- 2 safety eyes ½in (14mm)
- Polyester fibre filling
- Embroidery needle
- Scissors
- Stitch markers
- Sewing pins

COCKATIEL

Using A, work all stitches in a round from bottom to top. Stuff as you crochet.

Round 1: Make a MC with 12 dc (12 sts).
Round 2: (Dc, dc2inc) 6 times (18 sts).
Round 3: (Dc, dc2inc, dc) 6 times (24 sts).
Round 4: (Dc 3, dc2inc) 6 times (30 sts).
Round 5: Dc 25, (dc2inc) 5 times (35 sts).
Round 6: Dc in each st around (35 sts).
Round 7: Dc 25, (dc2tog) 5 times (30 sts).
Round 8: Dc 25, dc2tog, dc, dc2tog (28 sts).
Round 9: Dc 22, (dc2tog) 3 times (25 sts).
Fasten off and weave in the ends.
Attach B to the last stitch of round 9.
Round 10: Dc in each st around (25 sts).
Attach C to the last stitch of round 10.
Round 11: Dc 23, dc2tog (24 sts).
In the next round change to D for only the bobble stitch, then switch back to C for all of the dc stitches.
Round 12: Dc 12, BOB, dc 11 (24 sts).
Mark stitches 9 and 16 in round 12. These will be the 2 stitches where you will place the safety eyes later in the pattern.
Rounds 13–15: Dc in each st around (24 sts).
Place safety eyes on round 12 in the marked stitches. They should be 3 stitches away from the sides of the beak.
Round 16: (Dc, dc2tog, dc) 6 times (18 sts).
Round 17: (Dc, dc2tog) 6 times (12 sts).
Round 18: (Dc, dc2tog) 4 times (8 sts).
Fasten off and weave the yarn under each of the FLO, pull tight and hide the end inside the head.

TOP FEATHERS

Using C, work all stitches in a row.
After turning, work the dc stitches down the chains.
Do not cut the yarn but repeat this row twice to make 3 connected feathers.
Row 1: Ch 4, turn, dc in the 2nd ch from the hook, dc 2, ch 5, turn, dc in the 2nd ch from the hook, dc 3, ch 4, turn, dc in the 2nd ch from the hook, dc 2 (10 sts).
Fasten off and leave a long yarn tail for attaching later.

WINGS

Make 2 wings using A. Work all stitches in a round.
Round 1: Make a MC with 6 dc (6 sts).
Round 2: (Dc2inc) twice, (htr, tr) in the next st, ch 1, (tr, htr) in the next st, (dc2inc) twice (12 sts).
Fasten off and leave a long yarn tail for attaching later.

DETAILS AND ASSEMBLY

Pin the wings to the side of the body between rounds 6 and 9 and past the pink cheek detail. The point of the wings needs to be near the tail and the rounded end near the front of the body. Make sure both the wings are evenly spaced on the body. Whip stitch them on using the embroidery needle and the leftover yarn end from the fastening of the wing (see page 18). Start at the top, working around the rounded front half of the wing, but leave the back half of the wing not sewn. Weave the extra ends into the body.

Pin the top feathers centred on the head, beginning 5 rounds above the beak, between rounds 17 and 18, and ending between rounds 17 and 18 on the back of the head. Whip stitch them on, using the embroidery needle and the leftover yarn ends. Weave the extra ends into the body.

Details of how to outline the safety eyes and add the cheeks are on page 19.

TALLULAH THE TARANTULA

Tarantulas are low-maintenance, eight-legged furry pets that thrive in small, well-landscaped habitats. With lifespans over 20 years and various species and colours, they attract many admirers. However, feeding them might not be appealing to everyone; for this reason, Tallulah identifies as a vegetarian to avoid frightening her owner.

Finished size

5½in (14cm)

Supplies and materials

- Universal Yarn Bella Chenille, Super Bulky Weight, 100% Polyester, 131yds (120m) per 100g ball
  Yarn A Peach 115
  Yarn B Sesame 120
- Hook size: 3.5mm (UK9:USE/4)
- 2 safety eyes ½in (14mm) and 2 safety eyes ¾in (18mm)
- Polyester fibre filling
- Embroidery needle
- Scissors
- Stitch markers
- Sewing pins

TARANTULA

Using A, work all stitches in a round from front to back. Stuff as you crochet.

Round 1: Make a MC with 8 dc (8 sts).

Round 2: (Dc2inc) 8 times (16 sts).

Mark stitches 3 and 9 in round 2. These will be the 2 stitches where you will place the ¾in safety eyes later in the pattern.

Change to B for each of the BOB stitches in the next round, then switch back to A for the dc stitches.

Round 3: (Dc, dc2inc) 6 times, (BOB, dc2inc) twice (24 sts).

Round 4: (Dc 3, dc2inc) 6 times (30 sts).

Mark stitches 4 and 17 in round 5. These will be the 2 stitches where you will place the ½in safety eyes later in the pattern.

Round 5: Dc in each st around (30 sts).

Rounds 6–7: Dc in each st around (30 sts).

Add the safety eyes in the marked stitches on rounds 2 and 5. If the safety eyes are not even, adjust them by 1–2 stitches.

Round 8: (Dc 3, dc2tog) 6 times (24 sts).

Round 9: (Dc, dc2tog, dc) 6 times (18 sts).

Change to B on the last stitch of round 9.

Round 10: FLO (dc, dc2inc, dc) 6 times (24 sts).

Round 11: FLO (dc, dc2inc) 12 times (36 sts).

Rounds 12–14: Dc in each st around (36 sts).

Round 15: (Dc 2, dc2tog, dc 2) 6 times (30 sts).

Round 16: Dc in each st around (30 sts).

Round 17: (Dc 3, dc2tog) 6 times (24 sts).

Round 18: Dc in each st around (24 sts).

Round 19: (Dc, dc2tog, dc) 6 times (18 sts).

Round 20: (Dc, dc2tog) 6 times (12 sts).

Round 21: (Dc, dc2tog) 4 times (8 sts).

Fasten off and weave the yarn under each of the FLO, pull tight, and hide the end inside the head.

LEGS

Using A and B, work all stitches in a row.
Make 8 legs, 4 in each colour.
When turning, put the stitch in the 2nd ch from the hook.
Row 1: Ch 9, turn (9 sts).
Row 2: Sl st 3, dc2tog, sl st 3 (7 sts).
Fasten off and leave a long yarn tail for attaching later.

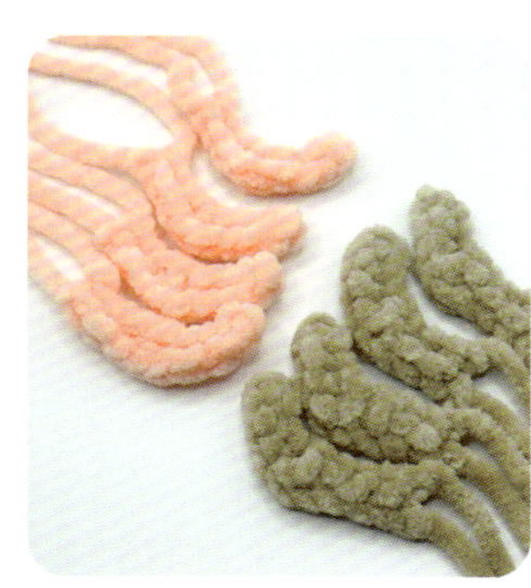

DETAILS AND ASSEMBLY

Pin the 4 Peach-coloured front legs to the sides of the tarantula's head, curving towards the front of the face. Starting on the right side, pin the 1st leg 2 stitches from the BOB stitch between rounds 8 and 9 and 2 stitches below the small safety eye. Pin the 2nd Peach leg along the same stitches just behind the 1st leg. Repeat the steps on the left side of the tarantula's head with the second pair of Peach front legs. Make sure the 4 legs are spaced evenly on both sides of the head before sewing. Whip stitch them on using the embroidery needle and the yarn ends from each of the legs. Knot both yarn ends together and weave them into the head.

Pin the 4 Sesame-coloured back legs to the sides of the tarantula's body but curving opposite from the front legs. Starting on the right side, pin the 1st Sesame leg between rounds 9 and 10 and lining up with the front 2 Peach legs. Pin the 2nd back Sesame leg along the same stitches just behind the 1st back leg. Repeat the steps on the left side of the tarantula's body with the second pair of Sesame back legs. Make sure the 4 legs are lining up on both sides the body before sewing. Whip stitch them on using the embroidery needle and the yarn ends from each of the legs. Knot both yarn ends together and weave them into the head.

Details of how to outline the safety eyes and add the cheeks are on page 19.

CHI CHI THE CHINCHILLA

The softest pet you can have is a chinchilla. They have incredibly dense fur that feels luxurious when you pet them, making them suitable for people who are allergic to some other animals. Chinchillas are quick, trainable and affectionate toward their owners. Our Chi Chi is a wonderful, soft and cuddly pet, specifically designed using fuzzy chenille yarn!

Finished size

6in (15cm)

Supplies and materials

- Universal Yarn Bella Chenille, Super Bulky Weight, 100% Polyester, 131yds (120m) per 100g ball
  Yarn A Misty 119
  Yarn B Blush 127
  Yarn C Sugar Plum 108
- Hook size: 3.5mm (UK9:USE/4)
- 2 safety eyes ½in (14mm)
- Polyester fibre filling
- Embroidery needle
- Scissors
- Stitch markers
- Sewing pins

CHINCHILLA

Using A, work all stitches in a round from bottom to top. Stuff as you crochet.

Round 1: Make a MC with 12 dc (12 sts).
Round 2: (Dc, dc2inc) 6 times (18 sts).
Round 3: (Dc, dc2inc, dc) 6 times (24 sts).
Round 4: (Dc 3, dc2inc) twice, dc, BOB, dc, (dc2inc) twice, dc, BOB, dc, (dc2inc, dc 3) twice (30 sts).
Rounds 5–7: Dc in each st around (30 sts).
The BOB stitches in the next round should be directly above the BOB stitches in round 4. If not, increase or decrease 1–2 stitches.
Round 8: Dc 11, BOB, dc 6, BOB, dc 11 (30 sts).
Round 9: Dc 9, (dc2tog) 6 times, dc 9 (24 sts).
Round 10: Dc 7, FLO (dc2inc) 10 times, dc 7(34 sts).
Rounds 11–12: Dc in each st around (34 sts).
Round 13: Dc 11, (dc2tog) 6 times, dc 11 (28 sts).
Mark stitches 12 and 18 in round 13. These will be the 2 stitches where you will place the safety eyes later in the pattern.
Round 14: Dc in each st around (28 sts).
Round 15: (Dc 5, dc2tog) 4 times (24 sts).
Add the safety eyes in the marked stitches on round 13. There should be 5 stitches between them.
Round 16: Dc in each st around (24 sts).
Round 17: (Dc, dc2tog, dc) 6 times (18 sts).
Round 18: (Dc, dc2tog) 6 times (12 sts).
Round 19: (Dc, dc2tog) 4 times (8 sts).
Fasten off and weave the yarn under each of the front loops only, pull tight and hide the end inside the head.

EARS

Inner ear

Make 2 inner ears using B. Work all stitches in a round.

Round 1: Make a MC with 12 dc (12 sts).
Round 2: (Dc, dc2inc) 6 times (18 sts).
Round 3: (Dc, dc2inc, dc) 6 times (24 sts).
Round 4: (Dc 3, dc2inc) 6 times (30 sts).
Fasten off and hide the tails inside the inner ear.

Outer ear

Make 2 outer ears using A. Work all stitches in a round.

Round 1: Make a MC with 12 dc (12 sts).
Round 2: (Dc, dc2inc) 6 times (18 sts).
Round 3: (Dc, dc2inc, dc) 6 times (24 sts).
Round 4: (Dc 3, dc2inc) 6 times (30 sts).
Place both the inner and outer parts of the ear together. Make sure both the wrong sides of each piece are facing each other. Dc the next round through both pieces of the ear, making them into one complete ear. Do not stuff.
Round 5: (Dc 2, dc2inc, dc 2) 6 times (36 sts).
Pinch the ear closed and dc across only the next 4 stitches connecting both sides, closing the bottom of the ear and creating a small seam.
Fasten off and leave a long yarn tail for attaching later.

TAIL

Using A, work all stitches in a round.
Stuff as you crochet.
Round 1: Make a MC with 6 dc (6 sts).
Round 2: Dc in each st around (6 sts).
Round 3: (Dc2inc) 6 times (12 sts).
Round 4: Dc in each st around (12 sts).
Round 5: (Dc, dc2inc) 6 times (18 sts).
Rounds 6–10: Dc in each st around (18 sts).
Round 11: (Dc, dc2tog) 6 times (12 sts).
Rounds 12–14: Dc in each st around (12 sts).
Flatten and crochet through both sides (6 sts).
Fasten off and leave a long yarn tail for attaching later.

DETAILS AND ASSEMBLY

Using pins, mark the width of the nose in the centre of the face between rounds 13 and 14, 2 stitches apart. With the embroidery needle and C, push the yarn through the side of the head to the first nose pin. Whip stitch a nose at the two pins at least twice, then add one centred whip stitch, 2 rounds below the nose and up to the bottom of the whip stitched nose (see page 18). Take the yarn back through the same stitch on the side of the head, knot the two ends, and weave the ends into the head.

Pin the ears to the side of the head between rounds 12 and 13, 3 stitches past the safety eyes. Make sure both the ears are evenly spaced on the head. When pinned correctly, whip stitch them on using the embroidery needle and the leftover yarn end from attaching the two ear pieces together. Sew along the seam, then bring the needle up through the head to round 16 and add a whip stitch to the front edge of the ear to secure it to the top of the head. Weave the ends into the head.

Pin the tail between rounds 2 and 3 of the bottom of the back of the body. This placement is so the tail will help the chinchilla sit up properly. Once centred, use the embroidery needle and whip stitch on the tail. Weave the needle through the back about 4 rounds up from where the tail is. Add an extra whip stitch or two to keep the tail in place at the back of the body, then weave in the end.

Details of how to outline the safety eyes and add the cheeks are on page 19.

HOUDINI THE HERMIT CRAB

Hermit crabs are small, land-dwelling crustaceans with soft bodies that need shells for protection. They live in tropical environments, so their habitat requires sand, fresh water, salt water, climbing structures, proper temperatures, humidity levels and extra shells for survival. Since they are social animals, you might want to crochet three or more hermit crabs like Houdini in fun colours and keep them together in one terrarium.

Finished size

4½in (11.5cm)

Supplies and materials

- Universal Yarn Bella Chenille, Super Bulky Weight, 100% Polyester, 131yds (120m) per 100g ball
  Yarn A Ripe Berry 107
  Yarn B Blush 127
- Hook size: 3.5mm (UK9:USE/4)
- 2 safety eyes ½in (14mm)
- Polyester fibre filling
- Embroidery needle
- Scissors
- Stitch markers
- Sewing pins

HERMIT CRAB

Using A, work all stitches in a round from bottom to top. Stuff as you crochet.

Round 1: Make a MC with 12 dc (12 sts).
Round 2: (Dc, dc2inc) 6 times (18 sts).
Round 3: (Dc, dc2inc, dc) 6 times (24 sts).
Round 4: (Dc 3, dc2inc) 6 times (30 sts).
Round 5: Dc, BOB, dc 3, BOB, dc 9, BOB, dc 3, BOB, dc 3, (dc2inc) 5 times, dc 2 (35 sts).
Round 6: Dc in each st around (35 sts).
Round 7: Dc 23, (dc2tog) 5 times, dc 2 (30 sts).
Round 8: (Dc 3, dc2tog) 6 times (24 sts).
Round 9: Dc in each st around (24 sts).
Round 10: (Dc, dc2tog, dc) 6 times (18 sts).
Round 11: (Dc, dc2tog) 6 times (12 sts).
Round 12: (Dc, dc2tog) 4 times (8 sts).
Fasten off and weave the yarn under each of the front loops only, pull tight and hide the end inside the shell.

ARMS

Make 2 arms using A. Work all stitches in a row. After turning, work the dc stitches down the chains. Do not cut the yarn but repeat this step to make the 2 connected claws.

Row 1: Ch 7, turn, dc in the 2nd ch from the hook, dc, sl st, ch 4, turn, dc in the 2nd ch from the hook, dc, sl st, then sl st again but into the starting sl st from the 1st claw, dc 3 down the original starting chain (10 sts).
Fasten off and leave a long yarn tail for attaching later.

SHELL

Using B, work all stitches in a round from top to bottom. Stuff as you crochet.

Round 1: Make a MC with 8 dc (8 sts).
Round 2: (Dc, dc2inc) 4 times (12 sts).
Round 3: BLO (dc, dc2inc) 6 times (18 sts).
Round 4: BLO (dc, dc2inc, dc) 6 times (24 sts).
Round 5: BLO dc in each st around (24 sts).
Round 6: BLO (dc 3, dc2inc) 6 times (30 sts).
Rounds 7–9: BLO htr 15, dc 15 (30 sts).
Round 10: BLO htr 15, FLO (dc, dc2inc) 7 times, dc (37 sts).

Fasten off and leave a long yarn tail for attaching later.

EYES

Make 2 eyes using A. Work all stitches in a round from top to bottom.

Do not stuff.

Round 1: Make a MC with 6 dc (6 sts).

Round 2: (Dc2inc) 6 times (12 sts).

Mark stitch 5 in round 2. This will be the stitch where you will place the safety eye later in the pattern.

Rounds 3–4: Dc in each st around (12 sts).

Add the safety eye in the marked stitch on round 2.

Round 5: (Dc2tog) 6 times (6 sts).

Round 6: Dc in each st around (6 sts).

Pinch the opening closed. If the seam is not horizontal with the safety eye, increase or decrease 1–2 stitches.

Dc through both sides with 3 dc and close the opening (3 sts).

Fasten off and leave a long yarn tail for attaching later.

DETAILS AND ASSEMBLY

Pin the eyes to the top front of the body between rounds 8 and 9, with 2 stitches separating them. The front section is rounded, and the back of the hermit crab is pointed. Make sure the eyes are evenly spaced and lined up between the front 2 bobble stitches. Whip stitch them on using the embroidery needle and the yarn end from closing each of the eyes (see page 18). Do not cut either yarn end.

Bring the embroidery needle up through the top of the body between rounds 9 and 10 and add an extra whip stitch to the lower back of the eye and the top of the body. This secures the eye in place without it flopping forward. Weave the extra end into the body and repeat this step for the second eye.

Pin the arms to the sides of the body between rounds 5 and 7, past the first bobble stitch and the bottom of the eye. Whip stitch them on using the embroidery needle and the leftover yarn ends. Weave the ends into the body.

To attach the shell to the hermit crab, pin it over the back with the FLO increases from round 10 centred on the top of the body. The sides of the shell should stop against the back 2 bobble stitches. Attach the bottom of the shell with whip stitches using the embroidery needle and the long yarn tail. Bring the embroidery needle up through the shell between rounds 9 and 10 and add 3 or 4 spaced whip stitches to secure the top portion to the body. Weave the ends into the shell.

Details of how to outline the safety eyes and add the cheeks are on page 19.

HOBBS THE HEDGEHOG

Hedgehogs are not cuddly pets! Shortly after they're born, their small bodies become covered with sharp quills, which serve as a defence mechanism since they are prey animals. However, this shouldn't deter you from considering these fascinating creatures for your next pet adventure. When our hedgehog, Hobbs, is not hibernating, he enjoys floating on his back during bath time, playing with empty toilet paper rolls and munching on mealworms or crickets.

Finished size

4in (10cm)

Supplies and materials

- Premier Yarns Parfait Chunky, Super Bulky Weight, 100% Polyester, 131yds (120m) per 100g ball
  Yarn A Shell 32
  Yarn B Teddy Bear 36
  Yarn C Chocolate 35

- Hook size: 3.5mm (UK9:USE/4)
- 2 safety eyes ½in (14mm)
- Polyester fibre filling
- Embroidery needle
- Scissors
- Stitch markers
- Sewing pins

Please note: when doing multiple colour changes in a round, you can either cut and tie off the colours after every change or leave a loose running stitch.

HEDGEHOG

Using A, work all stitches in a round from bottom to top. Stuff as you crochet.

Round 1: Make a MC with 12 dc (12 sts).

Round 2: (Dc, dc2inc) 6 times (18 sts).

Round 3: (Dc, dc2inc, dc) 6 times (24 sts).

Change to B for each of the bobble stitches in the next round, then switch back to A on the dc stitches.

Round 4: (Dc 3, dc2inc) 4 times, BOB, dc 2, dc2inc, dc, BOB, dc, dc2inc (30 sts).

Change to B on the last stitch on round 4, then switch back to A when instructed.

Round 5: (Dc 2, BOB) 5 times, dc 2, (change to A) dc 13 (30 sts).

Change to B on the last stitch on round 5.

Round 6: Dc 3, (BOB, dc 2) 4 times, BOB, dc 2, (change to A) dc 12 (30 sts).

Change to B on the last stitch on round 6.

Round 7: (Dc 2, BOB) 5 times, dc 3, (change to A) dc 12 (30 sts).

Change to B on the last stitch on round 7. The single bobble stitches in round 8 should line up with the bobble stitches in round 4. If they are not, adjust them left or right by 1–2 stitches to get the correct placement. These ones in front of the body are the feet.

Round 8: Dc 3, (BOB, dc 2) 5 times, BOB, (change to A) dc 2, (change to B) BOB, (change to A) dc 5, (change to B) BOB, (change to A) dc 2 (30 sts).

Change to B on the last stitch on round 8.

Round 9: (Dc 2, BOB) 6 times, dc, (change to A) dc 11 (30 sts).

Change to B on the last stitch on round 9.

Round 10: Dc 3, (BOB, dc 2) 4 times, BOB, dc 3, (change to A) dc 11 (30 sts).

Change to B on the last stitch on round 10.

The htr2inc in the next round should be centred between the 4 bobble feet stitches. If not, adjust them by 1–2 stitches.

Round 11: (Dc 2, BOB) 6 times, dc, (change to A) dc 5, (htr2inc) twice, dc 4 (32 sts).

Change to B on the last stitch on round 11.

Round 12: Dc 3, (BOB, dc 2) 4 times, BOB, dc 4, (change to A) dc 4, (dc2tog) twice, dc 4 (30 sts).

Mark stitches 23 and 29 in round 12. These will be the 2 stitches where you will place the safety eyes later in the pattern.

Change to B on the last stitch on round 12.

Round 13: Dc 2, BOB, (dc2tog, BOB) 5 times, dc 2, (change to A) dc 4, dc2tog, dc 4 (24 sts).

Change to B on the last stitch on round 13.

Round 14: Dc 3, (BOB, dc) 4 times, BOB, dc 3, (change to A) dc 9 (24 sts).

Add the safety eyes in the marked stitches on round 12. There should be 6 stitches between them.

Change to B on the last stitch on round 14.

Round 15: (Dc2tog) twice, (dc, BOB) 4 times, dc, dc2tog, (change to A) dc2tog, dc 5, dc2tog (19 sts).

Change to B on the last stitch on round 15.

Round 16: Dc, dc2tog, dc, BOB, dc2tog, BOB, dc, dc2tog, dc 8 (16 sts).

Round 17: (Dc2tog) 8 times (8 sts).

Fasten off and weave the yarn under each of the front loops only. Pull tight and hide the end inside the head.

EARS

Make 2 ears using A. Work all stitches in a round.
Round 1: Make a MC with 5 dc, ch, turn (5 sts).
Change to B on the last ch stitch on round 1.
Round 2: Dc in each st around (5 sts).
Do not close but fasten off and leave a long yarn tail for attaching later.

DETAILS AND ASSEMBLY

Using pins, mark the width of the nose in the centre of the face between rounds 11 and 12 and a stitch apart. With the embroidery needle and C, push the yarn through the side of the body to the first nose pin. Whip stitch a nose at the two pins at least 3 times (see page 16). Push the yarn back through the same stitch on the side of the head and knot the two ends. Weave the ends into the head.

Pin the ears to the side of the head between rounds 11 and 15, approximately 2 stitches from the safety eyes. Whip stitch them on using the embroidery needle and the leftover ends of yarn B. Weave the ends into the head.

Details of how to outline the safety eyes and add the cheeks are on page 19.

TANK THE TURTLE

Choosing a turtle as a pet can be overwhelming because there are hundreds of species to consider. When you bring a turtle home, you gain a long-term companion and the chance to create a calm and soothing environment. For instance, Tank the Turtle enjoys a serene habitat featuring waterfalls, basking areas and tropical plants. Plus, having a turtle like Tank can be the perfect way to help you unwind after a busy day.

Finished size

6in (15cm)

Supplies and materials

- Universal Yarn Bella Chenille, Super Bulky Weight, 100% Polyester, 131yds (120m) per 100g ball
  Yarn A Ocean 105
  Yarn B Coastal 128
  Yarn C Honeydew 104
- Hook size: 3.5mm (UK9:USE/4)
- 2 safety eyes ½in (14mm)
- Polyester fibre filling
- Embroidery needle
- Scissors
- Stitch markers
- Sewing pins

TURTLE HEAD

Using A, work all stitches in a round from top to bottom. Stuff as you crochet.

Round 1: Make a MC with 8 dc (8 sts).
Round 2: (Dc, dc2inc) 4 times (12 sts).
Round 3: Dc 3, (dc2inc) 6 times, dc 3 (18 sts).
Round 4: Dc in each st around (18 sts).
Round 5: (Dc, dc2inc, dc) 6 times (24 sts).
Mark stitches 8 and 18 in round 5. These will be the 2 stitches where you place the safety eyes later in the pattern.
Round 6: Dc in each st around (24 sts).
Round 7: Dc 3, (dc2tog, dc) 5 times, dc2tog, dc 4 (18 sts).
Place safety eyes on round 5 in the marked stitches, with 9 stitches between them, making sure that the increases are centred between each of the safety eyes.
Round 8: (Dc, dc2tog) 6 times (12 sts).
Rounds 9–10: Dc in each st around (12 sts).
Pinch the opening closed, if the seam is not horizontal with the safety eyes, increase or decrease 1–2 stitches. Dc through both sides with 6 dc and close the opening (6 sts).
Fasten off and leave a long tail for attaching later.

SHELL

Using B, work all stitches in a round from top to bottom. Stuff as you crochet.

Round 1: Make a MC with 12 dc (12 sts).
Round 2: (Dc, dc2inc) 6 times (18 sts).
Round 3: (Dc, dc2inc, dc) 6 times (24 sts).
Round 4: (Dc 3, dc2inc) 6 times (30 sts).
Round 5: (Dc 2, dc2inc, dc2) 6 times (36 sts).
Round 6: Dc in each st around (36 sts).
Fasten off and weave in the yarn ends.
Attach A to the back loop only of the 1st stitch of round 6.
Round 7: BLO dc 35, BOB (36 sts).
Round 8: (Dc 2, dc2tog, dc2) 6 times (30 sts).
Round 9: (Dc 3, dc2tog) 6 times (24 sts).
Round 10: (Dc, dc2tog, dc) 6 times (18 sts).
Round 11: (Dc, dc2tog) 6 times (12 sts).
Round 12: (Dc, dc2tog) 4 times (8 sts).
Fasten off and weave the yarn under each of the front loops only, pull tight and hide the end inside the shell.

FLIPPERS

Make 4 flippers using A. Work all stitches in a round from top to bottom.
Do not stuff.
Round 1: Make a MC with 6 dc (6 sts).
Round 2: (Dc2inc) 6 times (12 sts).
Rounds 3–4: Dc in each st around (12 sts).
Pinch the opening closed, dc through both sides with 6 dc and close the opening (6 sts).
Fasten off and leave a long tail for attaching later.

DETAILS AND ASSEMBLY

Hold the shell with the bobble stitch facing you and yarn B on top. Pin all of the flippers and the head between rounds 7 and 8 along the bottom Ocean colour of the shell. Pin the 1st flipper between stitches 2 and 7, skip stitch 8 then pin the 2nd flipper between stitches 9 and 14. The next 7 stitches (15–21) need to be skipped for attaching the head later. Pin the 3rd flipper between stitches 22 and 27 and the 4th between stitches 29 and 34.

Flip the shell upside down and whip stitch the flippers on using the embroidery needle and the leftover yarn ends from each one (see page 18). Weave the ends into the body.

Flip the turtle over and attach C to the front loop only of round 6 with a dc, making sure it is centred with the bobble tail stitch. Add an extra dc in the same stitch to create an increase. Dc2inc along the remaining 35 front loop only stitches on the same round. This creates an outer edge on the turtle's shell. Fasten off and weave the ends into the shell.

Pin the head between rounds 7 and 8 in the space skipped when attaching the flippers. Make sure it is evenly centred and lines up with the bobble stitch on the back of the turtle. Use the leftover yarn end from closing the head and the embroidery needle to whip stitch it into place. Bring the embroidery needle up through the top of the neck between rounds 9 and 10 to add an extra whip stitch to the yarn C edging on the shell. This secures the head in place against the shell.

Details of how to outline the safety eyes and add the cheeks are on page 19.

SLITHERS THE SNAKE

Snakes possess some fascinating abilities! Their tongues are designed for smelling rather than tasting, and their jaws can detect vibrations to sense approaching prey since they lack ears. Additionally, some species have heat vision, which allows them to see their prey both day and night. While some people may find snakes scary, Slithers hopes to become good friends with you all.

Finished size

8in (20cm)

Supplies and materials

- Universal Yarn Bella Chenille, Super Bulky Weight, 100% Polyester, 131yds (120m) per 100g ball
  Yarn A Lush Green 114
  Yarn B Daffodil 102
- Hook size: 3.5mm (UK9:USE/4)
- 2 safety eyes ½in (14mm)
- Polyester fibre filling
- Embroidery needle
- Scissors
- Stitch markers
- Sewing pins

Please note: when doing multiple colour changes in a round, you can either cut and tie off the colours after every change or leave a loose running stitch.

SNAKE

Using A, work all stitches in a round from top to bottom. Stuff as you crochet.

Round 1: Make a MC with 8 dc (8 sts).

Round 2: Dc 3, (FLO dc2inc) twice, dc 3 (10 sts).

Round 3: Dc 4, (dc2inc) 4 times, dc 2 (14 sts).

Round 4: Dc 4, dc2inc, dc, change to B dc2inc, dc, dc2inc, change to A dc, dc2inc, dc 3 (18 sts).

Round 5: Dc 7, change to B dc 5, change to A dc 6 (18 sts).

Mark stitches 7 and 14 in round 5. These will be the 2 stitches where you will place the safety eyes later in the pattern.

Round 6: Dc 8, change to B dc 3, change to A dc 7 (18 sts).

Round 7: Dc 9, change to B dc, change to A dc 8 (18 sts). Cut B and tie off.

Round 8: Dc in each st around (18 sts).

Add the safety eyes in the marked stitches on round 5. There should be 6 stitches between them. The yarn B stitches should be in between the safety eyes. If they are not, adjust the eyes left or right by 1–2 stitches to get the correct placement.

Add the stuffing in small amounts to shape the snout and the head.

Round 9: (Dc, dc2tog) 6 times (12 sts).

Rounds 10–11: Dc in each st around (12 sts).

Round 12: Dc 3, sl st 3, dc 3, htr 3 (12 sts).

Round 13: Dc 6, htr 3, dc 3 (12 sts).

Round 14: Dc 3, sl st 3, dc 3, htr 3 (12 sts).

Round 15: Dc 6, htr 3, dc 3 (12 sts).

Rounds 16–19: Dc in each st around (12 sts).

Round 20: Dc 5, htr 3, dc 3, sl st (12 sts).

Round 21: Sl st 2, dc 3, htr 3, dc 4 (12 sts).

Round 22: Dc 6, htr 3, dc 3 (12 sts).

Round 23: Sl st 3, dc 3, htr 3, dc 3 (12 sts).

Rounds 24–26: Dc in each st around (12 sts).
Round 27: Dc 7, dc2tog, dc 3 (11 sts).
Round 28: Dc, dc2tog, dc 8 (10 sts).
The yarn change on the next round should be on the bottom of the snake. If it is not, adjust the colour-change stitch by 1–2 stitches to get the correct placement.
Round 29: Dc 3, change to B dc 3, dc2tog, dc 2 (9 sts).
Round 30: Dc2tog, dc 7 (8 sts).
Round 31: Dc 5, dc2tog, dc (7 sts).
Round 32: Dc2tog, dc 5 (6 sts).
Round 33: (Dc2tog, dc) twice (4 sts).
Fasten off and weave the yarn under each of the front loops only, pull tight and hide the end inside the tail.

DETAILS

Details of how to outline the safety eyes and add the cheeks are on page 19.

ABOUT THE AUTHOR

Jacki Donhou resides in Maryland, United States. She learned to crochet after becoming a stay-at-home mum. After several years of following other people's designs, she decided to create her own. Inspired by her love of animals and cherished memories of her children's favourite toys from their childhood, Jacki has since gained a loyal following on social media. Many people have fallen in love with her unique and fun amigurumi designs. Driven by coffee, laughter and a passion for colourful yarn, Jacki continually seeks new ways to bring joy to others.

She is the author of the books *Yarn Cake Amigurumi* and *Crocheted Mythical Creatures* and co-author of *Crochet Christmas*.

INDEX

First published 2025 by
Guild of Master Craftsman Publications Ltd
Castle Place, 166 High Street, Lewes,
East Sussex BN7 1XU, United Kingdom
www.gmcbooks.com

ISBN 978-1-78494-717-0

The EEA authorised representative is
Authorised Rep Compliance Ltd.
Ground Floor, 71 Baggot Street Lower,
Dublin, DO2 P593, Ireland
www.arccompliance.com

A catalogue record for this book is available from the British Library.

Publisher Jonathan Bailey
Production Director Jim Bulley
Senior Project Editor Susie Behar
Design Manager Robin Shields
Editor Cath Senker
Design Ellie Smith
Photography Andrew Perris
Stylist Anna Stevens

Colour origination by GMC Reprographics
Printed and bound in China

ACKNOWLEDGEMENTS

Thank you, as always, to my amazing publisher, Jonathan Bailey, for having faith in me year after year. I'd also like to express my gratitude to the entire team at GMC Publications for their hard work in helping to create this book with me and bringing all my designs to life. A big shout-out goes to my life-saving pattern tester, Christina Krieger! Thank you for your time, dedication, late nights and those super early mornings. You have been my rock throughout this entire process.

To the wonderful people at Universal Yarns and Premier Yarns – thank you for providing the gorgeous yarns for these designs and for supporting my new book.

To my husband and life partner, Chris, you are my everything. The unconditional love and support you give me every day make my present and future brighter. To my perfect kids – Athena, Roger, Charlotte and Caleb – who will forever inspire me to keep creating, you make my heart full! I also want to thank my parents and siblings for continuing to be my cheerleaders with each and every book; I love you all forever. Lastly, to my oldest friends and the new ones I have recently made – thank you so much for being a part of my village.

To order a book, contact:

GMC Publications Ltd
Castle Place, 166 High Street,
Lewes, East Sussex, BN7 1XU,
United Kingdom
Tel: +44 (0)1273 488005
www.gmcbooks.com